From Christ to God

From Christ to God

A study of some trends, problems and possibilities in contemporary christology

DAVID G. A. CALVERT

EPWORTH PRESS   *London*

© *Epworth Press 1983*

First published 1983
by Epworth Press
All rights reserved

Enquiries should be addressed to
The Epworth Press
Room 195, 1 Central Buildings
Westminster London SW1H 9NR

7162 0391 X

Typeset by Gloucester Typesetting Services
and printed in Great Britain by
Richard Clay Ltd (The Chaucer Press)
Bungay, Suffolk

Contents

Contents

Contents

Preface

I wish to record my gratitude to the Fernley-Hartley Trustees for their invitation to deliver the Fernley-Hartley Lecture at the Methodist Conference of 1983. The text of this book has been prepared in response to that invitation.

The book is intended for as wide a readership as possible and the text itself is designed to be read by the non-specialist. For this reason, a few explanatory comments about the meaning of technical terms, and other aids, have been included in the footnotes. The bulk of the footnotes, however, provides a running commentary on the text and relates its thought to contemporary scholarship. The notes are there for the interest of those who wish to pursue further various subjects raised in the course of the book. Books frequently referred to are listed in the bibliography. I am aware that at many places issues have been raised that deserve much fuller treatment. It has not, however, been possible to provide that treatment here.

I wish to express my gratitude to those who have helped me in the preparation of this book. Raymond George read an earlier typescript and made many useful comments and suggestions. Graham Slater gave me both encouragement and advice in the task of preparing that longer typescript for publication. I am most grateful to them both for the generous and kind way in which they helped me. The responsibility for errors and inadequacies is of course my own.

My gratitude to my wife Margaret for all her advice and encouragement is considerable. Throughout the preparation of this book in the midst of a busy circuit life I have received the utmost support from her and from our daughters, Jan and Tig. Without their co-operation the task would not have been possible.

Headingley, Autumn 1982   David G. A. Calvert

Introduction

This study in contemporary christology argues that much of our christological thinking ignores that theological context which alone gives
christology its justification.

Generally speaking, nineteenth-century jesuology has been replaced by
twentieth-century christology. Nineteenth-century thought sought a
purely historical picture of Jesus based on the techniques of historical
investigation. It did not accept the doctrine of the incarnation as its
presupposition, but instead treated the life of Jesus as a purely human
life which developed in a human way. Although the twentieth century
saw a return to a more serious treatment of the New Testament statements
about Christ, in some fundamental ways the christology which replaced
the earlier jesuology has failed to recognize its theological task. This study
urges a return to theology as the only proper context for christological
study. For only in this way can a more distinctively Christian understanding of God emerge.

The book is addressed to an English society which hesitates to call itself
Christian, but which is clearly still deist. Many people have not abandoned
belief in God, but they do not know what kind of God to trust. The task
of the church is to identity more clearly the character of the one true God.
More particularly, this is the role of christology. It is to be the servant
of theology so that the world may believe. Some are still attracted to the
figure of Jesus (though which Jesus is something of a puzzle); some cling
to a vague undefined belief in God (though what he is like they fear to
hazard a guess). A theological christology seeks to speak to both. To the
one it says that the significance of Jesus lies not in himself but in the one
whom he reveals. To the other it says, 'Here is the God whom you seek;
he is to be seen in Jesus Christ.' In this way we avoid the errors, on the
one hand, of a Jesus cult and, on the other hand, of mere deism. For both,
theological christology is a liberation and becomes a gospel to proclaim.

Introduction

In expounding this, the present book is divided into three parts. First, we examine some of the main trends in recent christology. Second, we look at the way some of the most persistent problems are treated in modern thought. Finally, we turn to the sort of possibilities that emerge if christology is given the theological role for which it is designed.

PART ONE

Some Trends in Contemporary Christology

Introduction

The most important points that separate modern christology from classical christology have their origins in Schleiermacher's thought.[1] Schleiermacher severely criticizes the weakness he sees in the traditional doctrine of the one person in two natures. He alleges that these concepts are misleading and unintelligible. He protests against both the 'scientific character' and the 'suitability for ecclesiastical use' of the expression 'in Jesus Christ divine nature and human nature were combined into one person'. He therefore seeks to replace the 'divine being who comes down from heaven' with a 'perfected humanity in which deity was experienced'. Much twentieth-century christology echoes this approach.[2]

Modern christological development is also influenced by Hegel, who urges that we should view history as a process.[3] He develops an essentially evolutionary view of the universe, and includes history and religion within this framework. The central issue that confronts us today in Hegel's thought is still that of the meaning of process, and the questions that need to be asked of his christology are precisely those questions to be asked of more recent dynamic christologies. The chief of these is whether such christologies allow a position of uniqueness to one such as Jesus who is described as belonging within the process.

Ritschl also has influenced contemporary thought. He contrasts hellenized Christianity with the dynamic, historical faith of the early church and judges that the original gospel has been transformed into a static, speculative metaphysical theory. He sees the task of modern theology as finding a return to dynamic, historical, Hebraic thought. Much of contemporary christology adopts a similar position, particularly in echoing Ritschl's belief that an alliance between theology and metaphysics was a fundamental mistake. Ritschl's alternative is to speak of Jesus having the 'value' of God.[4] The question, addressed as much to contemporary christology as to Ritschl, is whether this language satisfies our religious needs and meets the demands of Christian theology.

I briefly recall the thought of Schleiermacher, Hegel and Ritschl to remind us that the problems we encounter in contemporary christology are not new.[5] They go back, in their present form, to the beginnings of historical and scientific criticism, and, in different forms, to the very earliest christological attempts.

In the first part of this book we shall be concerned with three trends in recent christology associated with the influence of these theologians. The trends I identify are, first, a stress on the humanity of Jesus and an approach to christology from below; second, the rejection of nature language,[6] with its consequent attack on the doctrine of the incarnation; and, third, a more dynamic approach to christology, seen in both process thought and in a revival of Spirit christology.

− 1 −

A Stress on the Humanity of Jesus and an Approach from Below

A stress on humanity

The foundation claim of christologies which stress the humanity of Jesus is that, whatever else he was, Jesus was a member of the human race in the sense that he was one man among others.[1] To describe this state, the phrase 'real humanity' is sometimes used to indicate that Jesus was a man like ourselves, whose humanity cannot be distinguished from ours, for to do so would be to deny the reality of his manhood.[2]

Using the language of classical christology, such humanity is described as *homoousios* with our own, meaning 'essentially the same as ours'. Such a use of the term *homoousios* is a deliberate rejection of docetism, that explaining away of the human character of the life Jesus lived. But its use is also a criticism of the thought of the early church, which, it is judged, failed in practice to affirm the actual humanity of Jesus because of its preoccupation with asserting his uniqueness. The pursuit of the latter is often termed a 'high' christology, but those who today assert that Jesus' humanity is *homoousios* with ours claim that a christology which takes the humanity of Jesus more seriously is the true 'high' christology.[3] Its criticism of the patristic age therefore is that although it did affirm the reality of Jesus Christ's humanity, it did not take it with sufficient seriousness.

Those who choose to begin christology with this assertion of his humanity determine by their choice the nature of the christological problem. That is, for such an approach the problem is that of identifying the sense in which 'the human life of Jesus of Nazareth was at the same time . . . the very life of God Himself'.[4]

Roots of this emphasis

What are the roots of this contemporary emphasis on the humanity of Jesus?

3

First, it is now clear that, to some extent, nineteenth-century theological liberalism survived the attack Barth made upon it. The fundamental concern with the historical Jesus that characterized such liberalism has resurfaced. This suggests a basic dissatisfaction with an emphasis on incarnation which gives little explicit attention to the real humanity of Jesus. Barth has himself been critical of the extreme change of direction he expounded. He has acknowledged that he was only partly right when he utterly discarded earlier liberalism, and was partly heretical in speaking of the 'wholly other' breaking in upon us 'perpendicularly from above', and in stressing the 'infinite qualitative distinction' between God and man.[5] But the christology with which Barth corrected his earlier emphasis is not a return to nineteenth-century liberalism. It is rather an exposition of the belief that 'in Jesus Christ there is no isolation of man from God or of God from man'. The weakness in Barth's early christology was perceived by his critics from the beginning, and so the fundamental change of direction initiated by him was in some cases either ignored or by-passed. In either case, the tide of liberalism was not entirely stemmed. Such liberalism seeks to present Jesus as our contemporary. This involves an emphasis on the humanity of Jesus. But whereas nineteenth-century liberalism thought it could recover the historical Jesus, much twentieth-century liberalism has judged this cannot be done satisfactorily or sufficiently.

Second, despite the form-critical judgment that the historical Jesus cannot be recovered, the emphasis on the humanity of Jesus has received support from New Testament scholarship.[6] For historical criticism sees Jesus as a man sharing a specific cultural situation and tradition, and recognizes the cultural base of his ministry, as well as attempting to specify the particular milieu in which he worked.[7] Moreover, arising out of the earlier negativism of the form-critical movement, the new quest for the historical Jesus draws attention to the humanity of Jesus through its assertion of continuity between the early kerygma and the preaching of Jesus. Although not always recognized, such a recovery of the teaching of Jesus inevitably leads to a consideration of Jesus as teacher, and perhaps even to the personality of Jesus, long thought to be forbidden ground.

Third, Marxist scholarship has emphasized that the genuinely historical Jesus must have stood in a specific relation to the culture of his time and place. For example, it is argued that Jesus was strongly affected by the ideas of his time and milieu, not only in the sense of ideas from the immediate social crisis that the country was going through in his lifetime, but also that he was deeply rooted in the centuries-old traditions of his country and people.[8] The conclusion of such an approach would seem to be that the more human, accessible and intelligible such a culturally conditioned Jesus is, the more likely it is that faith in him as the universal Christ came later, as an invention.[9] This is one of the key problems that such a stress on the reality of Jesus' humanity creates. For an emphasis on the ordinariness of the humanity of Jesus necessarily raises the question of how and why the confession of his divinity could properly have arisen.

Fourth, in our secular age, God-language as a whole has been severely challenged.[10] This makes any description of Jesus Christ as the second person of the Trinity unintelligible to many. For apologetic reasons, therefore, Christians have found it more profitable to speak of the man Jesus. In this way he has appeared more real, and any docetism implied by a stress on his deity has been avoided. We see here that a stress on the humanity of Jesus and the rejection of 'nature' language are closely related. It is partly the concern about the inadequacy of nature language that has encouraged the tendency to emphasize the humanity of Jesus.

Approach from below

To begin christology with a recognition of the humanity of Jesus is to engage in christology from below, as opposed to an approach from above which starts with an assertion of his divinity. To adopt either approach is to beg a question. But to begin from below, it is argued, is at least to start on sure ground, and thus is the better question to beg. For we know that Jesus was a man; we know this by the most decisive criterion of all: he died.[11]

It is possible to do christology from below fruitfully only if it is clear that what is being asserted is not merely an abstract principle. Christology from below recognizes Jesus as a distinct individual, a person with specific beliefs, hopes and values, all expressed in the thought and imagery of a particular time and society.[12] Christology from below invites a response to this particular historical man. Such insistence is clearly necessary, for there would be something odd about a position which starts from below but is doubtful whether we can know anything much about the life of Jesus. To do christology from below, therefore, is not to assert a christological principle; it is to engage in a serious and detailed examination of the biblical material about Jesus of Nazareth.

Although christology from below chooses not to start with an assertion of incarnation, this does not mean that it need not be its intention to move towards incarnational thought. For not to pursue an incarnational conclusion as far as the evidence suggests is to decline the challenge of christological thought. How to move from one position to the other is, however, one of the problems facing those christologies which begin from below. Some do so through the resurrection, asserting that belief in the divinity of Christ can be traced directly to the resurrection.[13] This extends the area of historical investigation and it becomes unclear whether such christology is still, strictly speaking, from below.[14]

The question is how people were first led to a recognition of, or an assertion of, the divinity of Jesus Christ. For unless some specific point of reference can be identified, it is not easy to justify following through an approach from below to an assertion of incarnation. Otherwise, either the claim to divinity is tacitly accepted throughout and merely brought out in an unproven conclusion, or the step from humanity to divinity is not convincingly taken.[15] One possible way through this dilemma is to argue that the disciples were able to 'recognize' God in Jesus Christ during his earthly ministry (not just after the resurrection) because of their previous knowledge of God from his revelation to Israel, as recorded in Jewish scripture.[16]

Two older approaches

This basic trend in contemporary thought – a trend which begins from below with the full humanity of Jesus – is not, however, universally accepted. Two older christological approaches continue to be asserted. One, the doctrine of *anhypostasia*, is very critical of the approach I have described. The other, the doctrine of *enhypostasia*, is more sympathetic to christology from below and, perhaps because of this, offers the more helpful criticism.

The anhypostatic approach seeks a way of ascribing to Jesus a real humanity without regarding him as having been a man like ourselves. The theory accepts the human nature of Christ, complete in both body and soul, but refers to it as that which the divine Word united to himself.[17] This means that the person, or the soul, of this human nature was not created; it was the pre-existent Word or Logos. The anhypostatic approach argues therefore that in Christ there is a new creation of manhood. It is in this sense that an anhypostatic approach sees Christ's manhood as impersonal.

Such an anhypostatic approach is strongly critical of those christologies which take as their starting-point human nature as it is known to us and then inquire what must happen to the divine Word if it is to be compressed within its limits. The difference between the two approaches is characterized in this way: christology from below is 'a degradation of the divine Person rather than an exaltation of the human nature'. On the one hand, christology from below is closely related to the rejection of nature language, and, on the other hand, anhypostatic thought is neo-Thomist. It sees christology as basically an ontological concern in which humanity is taken up into divine experience. 'Person' is not interpreted as a psychological concept but essentially an ontological one: in the incarnation God became man by taking mankind into himself. In reply, however, those who argue for a christological approach from below are deeply suspicious of any concept of impersonal humanity, arguing that 'it is nonsense to say that he is "man" unless we mean that He is a man', that is, a man like ourselves.[18] They are also sceptical of the possibility of expressing a full, real humanity in a christology confined to ontological terms, believing that it is bound to be docetic.

Others have revived the doctrine of enhypostasia.[19] In contrast to the theory of anhypostasia which asserts the impersonality of Christ's manhood (he was Man rather than a man), the theory of enhypostasia suggests that divinity possesses humanity within itself: Christ's humanity is not therefore so much impersonal as more fully personal. What is common to both theories is that they seek to assert the full humanity of Christ within the Chalcedonian framework and use the traditional language of classical christology. One of the most important early attempts to develop the thought of Chalcedon was made by Leontius of Byzantium, with whose name the doctrine of enhypostasia is traditionally associated.[20] He continued the struggle of Chalcedon by asking how, if each nature must have its hypostasis, one can confess two natures in one hypostasis. Leontius' solution was to argue that divinity possessed humanity within itself.

It is possible to use the concept of enhypostasia in a more general sense; that is, not just applied to Jesus Christ, but to humanity generally.[21] In this sense, it is used to suggest that 'being in, of and through God' is generally characteristic of the creaturely status of a human person. Enhypostasis would then mean 'the incorporation ... of the human person *into* the "person" (hypostasis) of God'.[22] Such a use highlights the creative presence of God in man, what Eastern thought refers to as man's lingering in God. God's being in a creature could even be termed a hypostatic union, if, in his being, God is seen as pure hypostasis. The purpose of such a suggestion is to draw attention to the truth that people are created by God and that man in particular can become aware of God's indwelling.

This illustrates how important is our understanding of man for any christological definition. For such an understanding of man opens up the possibility of using enhypostatic language in its more historical sense too. I refer to the possibility of describing the centre of Jesus' life as being in God, without any suggestion that he finds his centre outside himself. Such language asserts that a human life completely grounded in God is not any the less a human life. It does not result in the loss of any aspect of being truly human. Such thinking does not go very far in specifying the mode of the divine presence in Jesus, but it lays a foundation for that possibility without the traditional tension between humanity and divinity. For many christologies from above and from below share the assumption that humanity and divinity are so different that it is necessary to start from one side or the other exclusively. Enhypostasia offers a hint that such dogmatism is not necessary, but rather leads to all the traditional christological problems. The attraction of an enhypostatic approach, therefore, is that it shares the strong desire of those christologies from below to assert and preserve the real humanity of Jesus without excluding a simultaneous recognition of his divinity.

Assessment

Any assessment of the contribution of christology from below must take into account the way in which such christologies cope with a number of key questions. Chief among these are the role of the historical Jesus, the problem of confining christology to the earthly ministry of Jesus, the question of the uniqueness of Christ and the unity of his person. Each of these questions arises directly out of this approach.

Christologies from below deal with the problem of the historical Jesus in different ways. If they are allied to a methodological scepticism with regard to the historical Jesus, it is difficult to see if more than an abstract principle is being asserted, albeit a principle which says that the humanity of Jesus was historically and culturally conditioned. Form criticism has certainly raised the question of whether we know enough about Jesus to enable us to build a christology from his alleged humanity.[23] The sort of quest that nineteenth-century critics engaged in is not now thought to be possible. But we must still ask how much it is necessary for us to be able to affirm about the historical figure in order for him to bear the weight of theological significance that any movement from his humanity to his divinity demands. Some modern christology makes its appeal to Christ without seeking to establish roots in the historical Jesus. But we must seek a christology rooted in his ministry, for there can be no christology apart from the history of Jesus of Nazareth.[24]

8

Secondly, an approach from below, seeking as it does to establish the ordinary humanity of Jesus, tends to confine the evidence to the earthly ministry of Jesus and to ignore the resurrection. But the Christ of Christian theology is much more than Jesus of Nazareth's earthly ministry. Christology is concerned with the risen Christ, if it is to reflect the central New Testament belief. 'Only the Risen One makes possible the presence of the living person and gives the presupposition for christology.'[25] The danger of confining christology to the earthly ministry of Jesus has long been recognized: second-century Ebionism was rejected for this reason.[26] The result can only be limited jesuology, whatever its judgment about historical research. It can never become christology without moving beyond his earthly ministry and considering the resurrection. The problem is that many approaches from below fail to move sufficiently in the direction of christology.[27] Early christology began with the humanity of Jesus but quickly moved into incarnational language. Today we may need to begin with Jesus of Nazareth, but we also need to recognize that christology is possible only if we indicate a special presence or activity of God in Jesus Christ which does distinguish his humanity from what is merely normal and merely ordinary. The resurrection is an indication of this.

Thirdly, we have seen that a stress on the ordinary humanity of Jesus raises the question of the uniqueness of Christ. This is one of the more acute problems that arises if christology emphasizes the reality and normality of the humanity of Jesus and leaves, as some would suppose, the divinity to look after itself.[28] For if christology sets out from the human side, the uniqueness of Christ cannot be based on the incarnation of the Logos. Rather is christology from below forced to ask what is special about the human Jesus, and whether this special something requires the language of divinity. The more christology insists on the humanity of Jesus, the greater is the need for that humanity to be qualified in some way. For without some such qualification, or assertion of specialness, the humanity of Jesus could not sustain the universal role that Christian theology has assigned to it. One possible response is to speak of a transcendent anthropology: man and God are not fixed natures infinitely apart, but man transcends towards God, and Christ is the point at which the two come together. Such language is developed in order to assert the universal role of Christ, an assertion which involves the fundamental metaphysical problem of the relation of the particular to the universal.[29]

Finally, christology from below raises the question of the unity of Christ's person. For in traditional terms an emphasis on his manhood

9

encourages a distinction of the natures. This was the effect within the development of the early tradition How does our contemporary emphasis on the reality of Christ's manhood cope with this potential problem of the unity of his person? Often it does not see it as a problem. It is pre-occupied with the need to assert his manhood and therefore does not consider the question of the unity of the human and the divine as a vital issue. This is because its single-minded approach does not easily enable it to treat the divinity of Christ with the seriousness it was accorded by those who sought to emphasize the humanity of Christ in the Antiochene tradition prior to Chalcedon.

Conclusion

In conclusion, therefore, I suggest that, if a study of the identity of Jesus of Nazareth is to be christological, the question of his humanity is not merely a historical or anthropological matter. It is theological. For the function of christology is ultimately theological. Our consideration of the humanity of Jesus takes us to the question of nature language, and how, if at all, we can attribute divinity to Christ, and what sort of divinity we need to affirm. Some who start from a consideration of Christ's humanity conclude that all that is needed is an assertion of 'adjectival divinity',[30] that is, divinity as a quality Jesus displays rather than his essential nature. But such an approach fails to move through christology into theology; that is, it fails to make sufficient claims about Christ and his relation to God for any theological conclusion to follow. The very distinction between christology from below and from above has, if it can be maintained, important theological conclusions. 'What sort of understanding of God does such a distinction entail?' is a question not faced by this contemporary trend. I suspect that this is because much christology from below is basically atheological. It does not conceive its christology to be a tool of theology, and therefore it does not investigate the theological implications of its approach.

– 2 –

A Rejection of Nature Language and the Doctrine of Incarnation

Objections to nature language

The use of the term 'adjectival divinity' and the designation of much christology from below as 'neo-Arian'¹ raises the question of the relation of contemporary christology to classical christology. While some contemporary christology still sees its task as basically the elaboration of the dogma of Nicaea and Chalcedon, a clear trend has emerged against this approach. There are two features of this trend, namely, the rejection of nature language and objections raised to the language of incarnation. Some of the earlier rejections of nature language in modern christology attempted to retain the general notion of incarnation. More recently, however, the attack on classical christology has been more specifically directed against incarnational expressions.

We have noted Schleiermacher's influence in establishing many of the trends still working themselves out in contemporary christology, and, although sometimes rephrased, all contemporary rejection of nature language basically echoes Schleiermacher's objections. His contention is that the very use of the word 'nature' to refer to divine being as well as human places the problem of the incarnation in a false setting. For such terminology suggests that the incarnation means the coming together of two types of being within the same category. Divine and human, he argues, cannot be brought together under any single conception, 'for in one sense we actually oppose God and nature to one another, and hence in this sense cannot attribute a nature to God'.² He therefore concludes that what results from such an attempt is a vacillation between the error of mixing the two natures to form a third or of keeping the two natures separate, neglecting the unity of the person.

Contemporary criticism of nature language argues that the two-nature language does not take the concrete unity of the historical man Jesus as the given point but rather the difference between humanity and divinity:

11

Jesus appears as a being bearing and uniting two opposite substances in himself.[3] This is substantially the same as Schleiermacher's criticism, for it argues that the two-nature doctrine suggests that one person is supposed to participate in two wholly different natures, and concludes that there could be no vital unity without one nature giving way to the other. But, in its modern form, the criticism is not based solely on the use of the term 'nature' (which could appear to be a linguistic objection), but rests more firmly on the importance of the historicity of the man Jesus in whom humanity and divinity were united. The use of nature language, it is suggested, does not give sufficient importance to the historical categories found in the New Testament, categories such as conflict, temptation, ignorance and development.[4]

Not all contemporary criticism of nature language involves a rejection of the ontological perspective of christological formulations, nor of the thought of Nicaea and Chalcedon. On the contrary, Bonhoeffer sees the basic christological question as ontological: it is a question of the being of Christ. He argues that the traditional nature language fails because it seeks to answer the question 'how?' instead of 'who?'. He therefore accepts the value of Nicaea and Chalcedon both as illustrating the limitations of the concept of nature and as pointing to a different question: who are you?[5] This wish to evaluate the work of Nicaea and Chalcedon positively and yet to avoid the repetition of the problems of nature language has led, naturally enough, to the use of alternative expressions. These include the term 'entering the human situation', as an alternative to the traditional 'assuming human nature',[6] and the use of the terms 'Eternal God-Manhood', 'New Being' and 'Spirit', as replacements of an allegedly static essence by a more dynamic relation.[7]

A defence of nature language

The rejection of nature language, so common in contemporary thought, has not gone unchallenged. A more sympathetic view of its continuing value is gained from a recognition of its original function.[8] The doctrine of 'one person in two natures' arose as the only way there appeared to be out of the dilemma expressed by Celsus in about AD 100. He put the question of how Godhead and manhood could be united in the one Christ and suggested the dilemma of either docetism or a change in the Godhead, that is, either the incarnation is only a semblance, or the incarnation means the Godhead is changed.[9] Pertinent though contemporary criticism of nature language may be, a proper assessment will recognize the fundamental reason why the answer came to be framed in the way it was. It was a question of whether God had really entered history while still remaining God. This is still the basic issue which concerns theology today, and it is important that it should be seen as a theological issue, namely, an issue about God, to which a response was made in christological terms. From the beginning christology was a servant of theology, for talk about Jesus Christ was developed in order to preserve and express a fundamental truth about God.

Much of the present criticism of nature language is concerned with its alleged inability to express dynamic concepts. It is certainly true that the classical conception of God presents him as a substance and also as immutable. For this reason it is assumed that the one conception necessarily involves the other. It is on this basis that criticism is made of the static character of nature christology, and the search for more dynamic terms is undertaken. More recently, however, it has been argued that the idea that, if God is a substance, he must be an unchanging substance, is a mere product of association. From this it would follow that 'the description of God in terms of substance does not of itself prejudice the question of whether God is, or is not, involved in change'.[10] Correct though this argument may be, the product of association which it acknowledges is itself a powerful reason for seeking different language, so long as this search does not involve a rejection of the purpose and value of the more traditional language.

Scepticism about the incarnation

Despite the defence that has been made of the traditional concepts, contemporary christology, starting from below, has for the most part not only rejected nature language but has also expressed growing scepticism about the incarnation itself. Christology from above has the concept of incarnation at its very centre, as seen, for example, in the theology of Barth, who combines the event of incarnation with the language of the descent and ascent of the Son of God. Behind such incarnational thought there lies the doctrine of the Trinity. For the doctrine of the Trinity is framed to answer the question of how the second person of the Trinity has assumed a human nature. Difficulties of such an approach have been well noted in contemporary theology: it presupposes the divinity of Jesus Christ, instead of presenting reasons for it; it recognizes only with difficulty the real, historical man; it attempts the impossible in seeking to describe the event from God's view. It is therefore often concluded that our starting point must be the context of a historically determined situation.[11] Such christology does not presuppose the incarnation; on the

Substance

contrary, the tendency today to start from below has led in many cases, though not all, to an abandonment of the traditional doctrine of the incarnation.

A rejection of the language of the incarnation arises also out of a rejection of nature language. This is simply a reversal of the process in the early centuries where it was the attempt to express incarnational thought which led to nature language.[12] Today, a rejection of the language of Nicaea and Chalcedon has led to an abandonment of the concept of incarnation. This is because behind the rejection of nature language there often lies a rejection of the divinity of Jesus Christ, as traditionally conceived: 'The critical historian no longer sees both natures displayed in Jesus' life. He sees a purely human Jesus, a first-century man of God in the Jewish tradition.'[13] From such a judgment there stems the criticism of traditional incarnational christology as incoherent, unintelligible and self-contradictory. In its place it is argued that non-incarnational christology is quite sufficient to do justice to the figure of Jesus of Nazareth and to what God was doing through him.

The mythical character of the incarnation

It is evident, therefore, that two factors have led to recent rejection of the incarnation: the approach from below and the rejection of nature language. To these we must add a third, namely, the categorization of the doctrine of the incarnation as mythological.

Before we seek to determine the value of this description, it is as well to recognize that there are different sorts of myth. A distinction can be made first between incorrect science and various sorts of mythological stories. Next, it may be possible to distinguish between those mythological stories which offer an explanation of observed facts, those which present a dramatic expression of truths about man's predicament, myths of nature and, finally, imaginative descriptions of the supernatural.[14] In the light of such possible distinctions it is right to enquire into the nature of the alleged mythical character of the incarnation rather than simply to support or oppose the designation of the doctrine as mythological.

Here a suggested distinction between Christian and pagan mythology becomes important. Pagan mythology, it is argued, has no conception of one decisive event (much takes place, but nothing happens), whereas Christian myth expresses 'the idea of a unique and decisive event'.[15] There are two aspects to this distinction. The first is the claim that Christian myth refers to an event. Pannenberg, for example, builds much on the resurrection as an historical event. For him the myth of the resurrection is not just a way of expressing and preserving a religious and theological judgment about the relationship of Jesus Christ to God. It is an interpreted historical event. Although few today would question the historical existence of Jesus of Nazareth, much of the contemporary debate about Jesus Christ reflects a high degree of scepticism about the historical value of the material preserved in the New Testament documents. The second element in this description of Christian myth is the claim of uniqueness for the event. Traditionally understood, the doctrine of the incarnation expresses the claim that the figure of Jesus Christ was unique. To describe the doctrine of the incarnation as mythological is not necessarily to challenge this judgment.

We see, therefore, that the chief concern about the designation of the doctrine of the incarnation as mythological centres on the question of the objectivity of the event. This is because only if its objectivity is established can any theological interpretation be offered of the event. This is where the argument about what sort of myth the incarnation is becomes really important. Bultmann's understanding of the myth of the incarnation is that it supposes a two-storied view of the universe which, when rejected, means the rejection of the theological truth it sought to express.[16] He has appeared to make the early Christian proclamation so dependent on a two-storied view of the universe that the objective presence of God in history is dissolved along with the dissolution of that view of the universe. His existential understanding of myth has attempted to do away with that objective content so central to the New Testament.[17] Our response must be to reject any demythologization which does away with the substance of Christianity; it has on *a priori* grounds treated as false the claim that God appeared in our world.

In such a discussion of the objectivity of events mythically expressed, the question of literalness becomes important. If the myth is treated literally, it becomes indefensible. This is what Bultmann has done, and so has reduced the Christian myth to an absurdity. But this is largely a failure to understand the function and nature of myth. For the incarnation does not suppose a physical journey by a pre-existent figure, but rather God's acceptance of a human existence. We can recognize Bultmann's programme of demythologization as a brave attempt to free the biblical message from a world-view that modern man can not accept, but we must reject his understanding of myth. For he has failed to recognize the need for religious language to be expressed mythologically.[18] What is needed to achieve Bultmann's goal is not demythologization but deliteralization. This means not taking the symbols as literal expressions of events in space and time, yet retaining the factual, historical element, and building upon that a theological interpretation. Without these two features – the factual element and the theological interpretation – the Christian faith is dissolved.

In some ways, much of the argument about the mythical character of the incarnation is a distraction. Partly because of the variety of understanding of the term 'myth', it is not always clear what is at issue. It is true that some find it positively helpful to describe the incarnation as myth: it conveys mystery beyond human comprehension[19] and it attempts to peer beyond the limits of human knowledge.[20] But without a more generally agreed definition of myth, it is difficult to see the value of arguing whether the doctrine of the incarnation is to be termed mythological. Often, in fact, it is factors other than the understanding of myth which determine the judgment about how to talk of any possible transcendent reality.[21] Maybe therefore the description 'mythological' is better avoided for the incarnation, so that the more central issues of what is being claimed in the doctrine can be examined,[22] namely, its historical basis and the ways in which it is possible to understand the claim that God was present and active in the person of Jesus Christ. Certainly it is far from clear that a preoccupation with myth leads to a more positive understanding of these christological claims or to a deeper knowledge of God. This is because talking about the mythological nature of the doctrine of the incarnation is too far removed from the figure of Jesus: it is talk about the way of talking about the claim made for a historical figure.[23] As such it is, at best, an indication of the nature of religious language and, at worst, a distraction.

More positive possibilities

We have seen that three factors have led to a questioning of the incarnation: the approach to christology from below with a stress on the full and ordinary humanity of Jesus has by-passed the incarnation; the rejection of nature language has led to a questioning of the doctrine for which such language was developed; the designation of the doctrine as mythological has led to a dismissal of its claims. However, such approaches do not necessarily lead to a rejection of the incarnation.

It is possible, for instance, to start from below without any commitment to the traditional nature language and conclude with a statement of incarnation. Wolfhart Pannenberg, for example, judges that, although the dilemma of Antiochene and Alexandrian christological solutions is insoluble if christology is developed from the concept of the incarnation, christology from below can culminate in the assertion of the incarnation as its concluding statement.[24] His own christology sees the resurrection as leading to a recognition of Jesus' unity with God. His conclusion is that 'in Jesus, God himself has come out of his otherness into our world, into human form'. To take another example, John Austin Baker's route is different, but like Pannenberg he starts from below and concludes with the incarnation. Baker's study of the life and teaching of Jesus leads to the conclusion that they are 'the perfect revelation of what God is like'. The resurrection does play a role, but only as giving an authority to what has been discovered in his life, teaching and death. It is Baker's detailed examination of this that makes him conclude that the incarnation is 'the once-for-all, historical embodiment of the personal God in a particular human individual'.[25]

Assessment

We have now seen some examples of this second trend in contemporary thought, a trend critical of nature language and the concept of incarnation. What preliminary conclusion can be drawn, and in what ways has this trend helped our understanding of the christological task today?

One criticism of such christologies is that they tend to be reductionist: they reduce christology to anthropology, the divine Son of God to a mere man, his ontological divinity to an adjectival divinity. How is such criticism to be evaluated? What is needed is a clearer set of criteria which can be used to determine whether a restated christology is fulfilling its proper role. At the conclusion of Chapter 1 I argued that a christology which put all its emphasis on the humanity of Jesus was in danger of attempting christology outside a theological context. This basic theological criterion can be applied here too. Unfortunately, much modern christology has done little to restore this theological framework, yet without it christology has no theological value. It is true, as we have seen, that a christology which chooses categories other than 'nature' and adopts a framework other than 'incarnation' may still seek to fulfil this theological requirement. But if such christology fails to be theological, it has become reductionist. A unitarian position prevents christology from influencing our understanding of God. For only a christology which recognizes God in Christ, whether it starts from below or above, is able to have theological influence, that is, able to influence our understanding of God.

My chief concern in this book is that much modern christology is in danger of neglecting its theological role. One of the most significant features of the Chaledonian definition is the importance it gives to the

immanence

theological setting of christology. Its aim is to preserve both divine transcendence and divine immanence. This theological context for christology needs to be preserved and reasserted today.

A second matter concerns the historical Jesus. For much of the rejection of traditional nature language as a description of Jesus Christ implies that it is possible to give a much more ordinary description of the human life of the man Jesus of Nazareth. It is at this point that the trends I have discussed in these first two chapters are most intertwined: both are caught up in the problem of wanting to affirm in principle what is, in principle, the subject of much scepticism, namely, the actual human life of Jesus. For, whereas Pannenberg and Baker, for example, are prepared for their approach from below to be dependent on a study of the historical Jesus, it is clear that the English mythologists are not. For their scepticism is not just about the incarnation. It extends to the historical study of the life of Jesus too. What then is the basis of their christology? It is neither a belief in the incarnation nor a study of the life of Jesus. It appears to be neither from above nor from below. Their criticism of these approaches is not matched by a positive account of any alternative basis for christology. Nor is it possible to provide one, without a more positive evaluation of the historical life of Jesus.

Appendix

We have seen that difficulties with the nature language of Nicaea and Chalcedon and with the doctrine of the incarnation have led to the abandonment of both. There have, however, been other reactions. I briefly note three: some have sought to defend the traditional formulations; some have used kenotic thought to express their meaning; some have sought an alternative metaphysical expression.

First, some still defend the doctrine of the incarnation in its traditional form. What is offered in such a defence, for example by Hebblethwaite, is neither a defence of an omniscient incarnate one, nor a defence of a literalized version of the myth of the incarnation.[26] Instead, it is argued that the notion of the God-Man is not a contradiction (we do not know sufficient of what it is to be God to be able to say that it is logically impossible for such a being to be incarnate), but rather expresses a fundamental belief which must be retained. This is the belief in a direct, personal encounter between God and man, made possible, it is argued, only by the Son of God's coming among us.

Second, kenotic christology, the theory of the self-emptying of God in Christ, is used to explain and defend a literal reading of the incarnation in suggesting *how* it was possible for God to become man.[27] Its commendable intention is to express an alternative to the choice between a docetic Christ and a human Jesus. But in treating the myth of the incarnation literally, it has failed to recognize the problems of the traditional formulation. The theory is an instance of reformulating a solution to the same problem (*how* God became man) rather than providing a solution to a reformulated problem.[28] For its reaction to criticism of a literal understanding of the incarnation is to seek refuge in a further degree of literalization.

Third, some have sought an alternative metaphysics on the grounds that much of the suspicion of the doctrine of the incarnation has arisen from the collapse of traditional metaphysics as a result of the development of modern science. The most powerful ideas of modern science arise out of the theories of evolution, indeterminism and relativity. Such ideas, it is argued, are not inherently anti-metaphysical: they attack traditional Western metaphysics but not, for instance, the Whiteheadian understanding of metaphysics. As, however, the true background to the language of Nicaea and Chalcedon is Greek metaphysics, not the ancient near-eastern myth of a pre-existent, descending and ascending heavenly being, it is possible to express the metaphysical language of the incarnation in terms which do not conflict with modern science.[29] In Whiteheadian metaphysics, incarnation is retained as a powerful and appropriate expression of God's self-giving love through Jesus Christ. This subject of process thought is taken up in the next chapter.

— 3 —

A Dynamic Approach: Process Thought and Spirit Christology

Introduction

Our third trend, a dynamic approach, is a response to the allegedly static character of traditional nature language. For one of the objections to the two-nature model is its concept of human nature as static, and the inference that this was what Jesus assumed at the incarnation. A more dynamic approach also reflects a desire to return to Hebraic thought-forms, and therefore arises out of a greater concern for biblically based theology. But more important than either of these factors is that a dynamic approach is an attempt to see how the Christian faith can be understood in a world dominated by the idea of evolution. The dynamic trend that has emerged in response to these influences has two principal strands within it. The first makes use of process philosophy; the second is Spirit christology.

Process thought

The process philosopher Whitehead describes reality as dynamic rather than static: man is on the move; the world of nature is evolving.[1] The result is a philosophy which sees reality as essentially dynamic, a rich complex of societal inter-actions in which whatever is actual is in process. Such an approach necessarily affects theology, and it is argued therefore that, since God is no exception to ultimate metaphysical principles, at least in some respects 'his reality must be described in terms of temporal events, processes and interactions'.[2] Process theology also judges that the description in traditional christology of the distinctiveness of God's presence in Jesus entailed a denial of his full humanity. It is argued that this was caused by the requirement of substance metaphysics that, if the divine Logos were present in Jesus, then some part of his human nature had to be displaced.[3] Process thought seeks to provide a more satisfactory basis for holding together the full humanity of Jesus and his distinctive relation to God.

At first, the christological implications of such thought were expressed only in general terms.[4] Divinity is described not as the privilege of standing beyond all suffering, but as sharing in it. This is based on a panentheistic view of God (that is, one which sees God in everything), which does not see him as unchanging essence but rather as one who completes himself in advancing experience. Such a view of God is an explicit alternative both to traditional theism and to atheism. When this view of divinity is applied to christology, Jesus becomes the supreme symbol of a God who is genuinely and sympathetically receiving into his own experience the suffering as well as the joys of the world.

The earliest sustained attempt to express the incarnation using process thought recognizes evolution as a necessary conclusion of modern science and so chooses evolutionary thought and the language of the philosophy of nature as an apologetic support for traditional christological views.[5] Man is seen as the organic summation of an unfinished process, the cosmic series, and Christ is seen as the one who fulfils history by entering it from beyond. There is therefore, it is argued, a finality in Christ's redeeming action in history: Jesus Christ is absolute actuality incorporated into history in the form of concrete individuality. This means that Christ is not seen as a product of history, a product of creative activity. Rather he is seen as the Logos-Creator self-incorporated into the series. The organism of Christ is a new creation, the organ adequate for the expression of his deity.[6]

But a more thorough-going application of process philosophy rejects any suggestion that the particular event of Christ is of an entirely different order from all the rest of the divine revelatory activity in creation.[7] It sees an insistence that the whole Logos is intruded into the world at the incarnation as a denial of the principle of process. For in securing the uniqueness of Christ, such a view demands a break in the series and so fails to secure sufficiently his ordinary humanity.

A greater reliance on process philosophy means following Whitehead's insistence that God is the chief exemplification of metaphysical principles rather than an exception to them. From this it follows that the power and love of God came to Jesus Christ not through some unique, unknown channel, but through prayer and self-commitment. Prayer is seen as a way of 'prehending' God; Jesus prehended God unreservedly. Such a view raises the question of the uniqueness of Christ, and it is argued that the divine co-operation in the case of Jesus was superior in duration and in degree but not in essential character.[8] The concept of immanence in process philosophy is used to describe the divine indwelling in Jesus

Christ as an example, indeed the chief example, of God's indwelling in his creatures. God's purpose for all men is to prehend God, but this was complete and permanent only in Jesus, for Jesus 'intensified his obedience' to God's call. Such a description is not meant to isolate Jesus from what went before or from the consequences of his life. Rather is the incarnation seen as a total complex of events with Jesus of Nazareth as the centre of that activity.[9] Within this total complex, however, the activity of God in Jesus Christ is seen as of decisive importance, providing a clue to how God acts in the world. He is not an anomaly, but the classical instance which discloses that God is pure unbounded love and that man is meant for love too.

Comparison with similar thought

Some further reflections on process christology can be gained by looking at the thought of two other theologians, Teilhard de Chardin and Karl Rahner, neither of whom embraces process theology, but both of whom seek a christology in line with an evolutionary view of the world.

Teilhard's presentation of the Christian faith expresses a close relationship between creation and incarnation.[10] The result is a more cosmic Christ than christologies from below produce. For Teilhard does not see the real significance of Christ lying in a mere humanity: why, he asks, should we turn to Judaea two thousand years ago if all we want is to cherish a man? While he recognizes the importance of the Jesus of history ('nothing appears except by birth'), it is in the more cosmic passages of the New Testament, particularly Colossians, that Teilhard sees the significance of Christ. He presents Christ as the alpha and the omega: 'he is the one who consummates all things . . . it is towards him and through him, the inner life and light of the world, that the universal convergence of all created spirit is effected in sweat and tears.' Evolution, he argues, took a new turn with Jesus Christ, who is the first of a new species of humankind. This was a spiritual, not a biological, development.

Teilhard shares the biblical conviction that all things were moving towards a culmination, and argues that the incarnate Christ carried out the functions of omega. This eschatological dimension leads Teilhard to view Christ not just as the culmination of a process, a new form of evolving humanity, but from the other side too, that is, the side of the eschaton. He insists that the omega was supremely present in Christ, and had to be if it was to be supremely attractive. Christ is therefore the centre of the evolutionary process, because he reflects the omega point into the heart of the process, and assures us of its reality by actualizing it in our midst.

Throughout his theological writings, Teilhard struggles to indicate ways in which his scientific view of the world can provide a proper context for theological belief and indeed bring about a clearer understanding of classical theological claims. For it was always his intention to present a balance between his scientific understanding of the world and his belief in what Christian tradition confessed about Jesus Christ. He argues that the universe cannot be bicephalic. However supernatural may be the synthesizing operation attributed by dogma to the incarnate Word, he argues that 'it cannot be effected in a divergence from the natural convergence of the world'.[11] He is anxious to assert that the universal Christic centre, determined by theology, and the universal cosmic centre, postulated by anthropogenesis, must ultimately coincide, or at least overlap. He judges it proper, therefore, that what is postulated by his scientific studies should be used to elucidate what is claimed by the dogmas of the church, and should be used also to take the dogmatic claims further than was possible in the cultural and scientific context in which they originated. His aim is to articulate a christology which will be in keeping with the dimensions of the universe as we know them today.

In each of these three respects Teilhard's thought is a useful complement to process christology. It expresses the notion of a cosmic Christ, while at the same time seeking to preserve his humanity. It sets christology in an eschatological context, almost entirely lacking in other forms of dynamic christology. It relates christology to science in a more explicit way than does process thought.

Rahner explores ways in which orthodox christology, to which he is committed, can be expressed through the vehicle of evolutionary thought.[12] He does not wish to present the formula of Chalcedon simply as the end of christological discussion. For him it is both an end and a beginning. He therefore welcomes the attempt to state christological belief in the context of creation, and suggests that categories taken from a truly theological doctrine of creation might be used to make the basic initial statement of what Christ really is. On the one hand, therefore, he speaks of the evolution of the world towards Christ, showing how a gradual ascent reaches a peak in him. On the other hand, he warns against any suggestion that this evolution is a striving upward of what is below by its own powers. Christ, he maintains, is 'the mysterious goal of God's plan and activity for his creation'.

In presupposing an evolutionary view of the world, Rahner describes man as the being in whom there is a breakthrough in the relationship

23

between matter and spirit. The incarnation is then seen as a necessary and permanent beginning of the divinization of the world as a whole. The incarnation is both a moment of God's communicating himself to the world and a part of the history of the cosmos itself. This means that the key to the incarnation is not God becoming human or man but God becoming material. Creation and incarnation are two moments in the same process of God's self-expression into what is other than himself. Rahner suggests therefore that, although the hypostatic union is in its nature a unique event, it is nevertheless 'an intrinsic factor of the whole process of the bestowal of grace on the spiritual creature in general'; in short, it is intended for everyone. Its finality, in his eyes, lies in its being God's absolute self-communication for the whole of humanity.

In seeing creation and incarnation as a question of matter and spirit, and in judging the incarnation as part of God's plan for all mankind, Rahner crystallizes elements in process thought and expresses them in a clearer theological context. But in deliberately refusing to embrace a particular philosophy, such as process, Rahner questions the role process philosophy should be allowed to play. Process philosophers believe that Whitehead's philosophy of internal relations provides a metaphysic in which subjects are internally related, without compromise to the autonomy of either subject.[13] Despite the attractiveness of this philosophy, Rahner has no desire to tie the church's doctrine once more to a particular philosophical framework. Because of this he is freer to explore, for example, the whole notion of 'becoming' (which he understands as 'self-transcendence'),[14] and the difficulties attached to the notion of God changing (which he does by distinguishing between God changing in himself and God himself being subject to change in something else).[15] His first commitment is to the Christian faith, not to a particular philosophical approach.

The approaches adopted by Teilhard de Chardin and Rahner serve to underline some important features prominent in process christology. Chief among these is the close relationship between creation and incarnation: a new approach to cosmology demands a new approach to christology. This perspective in turn raises the question of how God acts in history, both in creation and in incarnation.[16] Are these special acts of God in space and time? Is the event of Jesus Christ the decisive act of God in history? The merit of the approaches we have been discussing is that they enable the question of the uniqueness of Jesus Christ to be seen as a question concerning God and the uniqueness of his activity. Evolutionary christology has in fact helped to re-assert the theological nature of christology, for it is concerned first and foremost with the issue of God's relationship with his creation. Christology is not therefore seen as an isolated subject, but as an aspect of the question of God's creative and revelatory relationship with the world.

Spirit christology

Spirit christology, the description of Jesus Christ as one who was possessed by the Spirit of God, becomes an attractive model in certain circumstances. For example, sympathy with a dynamic way of viewing reality and an understanding of Jesus as an inspired man can readily be accommodated in Spirit christology. We have already seen that a dynamic understanding of creation need not be expressed in process terms. Other concepts can be used to describe a balance between change and constants in reality. But, to take one example, the term 'moving pattern' is hardly adequate for the incarnation, as it lacks reference to the life experience of Jesus.[17] So the phenomenon of inspiration is used as a more personal description of one whose life was under the influence of God. But because inspiration suggests an intermittent and perhaps temporary phenomenon, the category of Spirit is used to overcome these characteristics. Jesus is therefore described as the completely inspired person who is the temporal manifestation in a human life of the Word or Spirit of God.

It is clear that such a christology begins with the human rather than the divine. It speaks about a genuine man being possessed by the Spirit of God. Nevertheless, Spirit christology claims to express the same values as Logos christology, and denies that it is an inferior expression of God's presence in a human life.[18] It is a term, however, which, it is claimed, is able to accommodate itself to the human limitations of Jesus more easily than Logos christology. This is because it does not so readily suggest two centres of consciousness, human and divine, but rather one centre or unitary consciousness, which was human but in the very closest contact with the divine.

Clearly there are some difficulties attached to such Spirit christology. One such concerns the uniqueness of Christ. It is more difficult to assert absolute uniqueness in the context of a Spirit christology than in a Logos christology. The one suggests a difference of degree, the other one of kind. This raises, too, the criticism that Spirit christology is adoptionist: a human life has been adopted by the Spirit of God. A possible response is to argue that the human spirit was united to the divine spirit from the beginning. But, in turn, this leads to enquiry about the nature of the union. It is not sufficient to claim that there is a union between the human and divine spirit in Jesus without developing some theory of how such a union is to be expressed. On the face of it, the problem of the relation of the particular to the universal still remains. Aware of some of these difficulties, we can approach two particular examples of Spirit christology in order to evaluate its contribution.

Tillich's thought

Although Tillich's systematic thought is based on a theology of Being and New Being, he states that it is the Spiritual Presence in the Christ which makes him the centre of history. He further argues that christology is not complete without pneumatology, 'because "the Christ is the Spirit" and the actualization of the New Being in history is the work of the Spirit'.[19] In making this change from Being to Spirit,[20] Tillich is not just changing the category he uses to speak about Jesus Christ. He recognizes that the category he selects for christology is also the category to be used in speaking about God. This insight is fundamental to the relationship between christology and theology, and affects our whole understanding of the function of christology. For christology is not an end in itself. It influences our understanding of God, and so has a theological role to play. In Tillich's case, the development of a Spirit christology both illustrates and encourages his growing preference for a description of God himself as Spirit.

Tillich does not, however, embrace Spirit christology exclusively. His intention is to use it to balance a Logos christology.[21] The reason he does not reject Logos christology is 'because of the universalistic element it brings into the assertion that Jesus is the Christ'.[22] Of even greater importance than this, however, is the need Tillich sees to preserve the Jesus-character of the event Jesus as the Christ. His protest is against docetism. Spirit christology, in claiming that it was the presence of the Spirit that made him the Christ, enables him to do this. But he is clear that it is the divine, not the human, Spirit of the man Jesus which makes him the Christ: 'it is the Spiritual Presence, God in him, that possesses and drives his individual spirit.'[23] Tillich's intention is always to prevent his christology from the errors of denying either the Jesus-character or the Christ-character of Jesus as the Christ, that is, to preserve and restate the basic dogma which he judges was inadequately expressed in Nicaea and Chalcedon. He judges that no one single model is sufficient for this task, and therefore complements Logos christology with Spirit christology. For the awesome task of christology is not just to describe who Jesus is, but to find a satisfactory way of indicating the character of God himself.

Tillich asserts the uniqueness of Christ through the use of the phrase 'without distortion' when speaking of the presence of the Spirit.[24] The phrase indicates that it is the presence of God which makes him the Christ. But at the same time Tillich is anxious to set the event of Jesus as the Christ within the context of world history. He therefore describes Jesus as the Christ as 'the keystone in the arch of spiritual manifestation in history'. By this he means that the event of Jesus as the Christ is a unique event, but in no way isolated from other events in which the Spirit is working in people who are grasped by the Spiritual presence. On the other hand, he asserts that there will be no new manifestation of the Spirit in history which goes qualitatively beyond Jesus as the Christ. Taken together, these constitute for Tillich the meaning of Christ as the centre of history.

Lampe's thought

The way in which Lampe expresses the christological question is related to the answer he gives, for question and answer govern each other. He asks the double question: 'What is the relation of Jesus to God and what is his relation to Christians here and now?'[25] It is because Lampe expresses the former question in the context of the latter that he approaches christology by way of the concept of the Spirit of God. For he argues that, although in the New Testament 'Word' and 'Wisdom' language was used to express the conviction that Christ encountered men from the side of God, a different language was needed for the corresponding interpretation of the relation between Christ and believers. Lampe, therefore, is not just wanting to approach christology from below in the sense of starting with the humanity of Jesus. He is much more concerned with providing a christological framework in which he can relate present experience of Jesus to the experience of God who was in Jesus, and who is therefore the object of christological reflection in both the New Testament and the whole subsequent Christian tradition.[26] For Lampe argues that the task of christology is to explore the way in which God, as he is encountered in our life in Christ, is identical with Jesus the Galilean teacher.

The most significant aspect of Lampe's Spirit christology is his concept of God as Spirit. For, when Lampe speaks about the Spirit inspiring Jesus, he does not refer to a divine hypostasis distinct from God the Father and God the Son, but rather to God himself as active towards and in his human creation. He is speaking of God disclosed and experienced as Spirit in his personal outreach.[27] Lampe is right in judging that this is the proper way to expound Spirit christology, arguing as he does that it follows from the basic conviction that in Jesus Christ God himself has acted. Spirit christology is able to express this foundation stone of christology only if God himself is described as Spirit, for no adequate account can be given of Jesus unless God-language is applied to him. Lampe's use of the term 'Spirit', therefore, has to be understood within his definition that 'the Spirit of God is God disclosing himself as Spirit . . . transcendent God becoming immanent in human personality'.[28] He bases this on his reading of the New Testament where, he argues, God's active presence is understood in terms of Christ, and 'to experience God as Spirit and to experience the presence of Christ were one and the same thing'. It becomes clear, therefore, that Lampe does not present so much a Spirit christology as a Spirit theology, and shows how interrelated christology and theology are.

Lampe's inspirational model is not, however, an abandonment of the incarnation. He recognizes that if inspiration were understood as an impersonal influence, communicated to a human person externally by a remote deity, it would be inadequate to express the person of Christ, for it would lack the deeper meaning of the real presence of God. His Spirit christology, based as it is on a theology of God as Spirit, unambiguously affirms the real presence of God and thus intends to express what is most valuable in the concept of the incarnation. More than this, Lampe hopes that through the use of inspirational language he is able to overcome the inadequacy of an incarnational theology which reduces the union of God and man to a less than fully personal level. Yet he raises the inspirational model to a new level, giving to it an ontological dimension: it is God himself who is present in Jesus Christ.[29]

In developing his model of inspiration, Lampe argues that properly speaking the term Spirit refers not to God's essence but to his activity, by which he means God's creativity. This expression of christology in the context of continuous creation is one of the strengths of the description of God as Spirit, for it enables the question of what it was that God did for man in Jesus Christ to be part of the larger question of our understanding of God's activity. Lampe's answer is that in Jesus Christ 'God brought the process of creation to the point where man appears for the first time in the perfection of his proper relationship to God.'[30] It is clear, therefore, that, although Lampe speaks of a continuous and unbroken process, he wishes to assert that within this process there is a central and focal point at which we discover the key to the meaning of the process as a whole. For although he interprets the life of Jesus Christ as part of a process of God's activity, he does not wish to detract from the significance of the historical life of Jesus of Nazareth. It was through this life that the experience of God's acceptance of man into sonship came, and as a result of this life that the Christian community began. This was possible only because 'in him the indwelling of God was complete, and man's spirit, human personality, was perfected'.[31]

Assessment

We can assess the value of Spirit christology through asking two basic questions, questions which relate to the humanity and divinity of Christ. First, is it an adequate description of the human life of the historical figure, Jesus of Nazareth? It is possible to give a psychological response to this question, arguing that the concept of inspiration does no damage to a person's humanity but rather makes him more fully man, a person after God's image.[32] The way inspiration works, it may be argued, is that a person seeking the intention and will of God would find the insight and power given within himself. But quite apart from such a psychological account, which would not appeal to those sceptical about recovering the historical Jesus, it is clear on other grounds that the concept of inspiration does not damage the humanity of Jesus. For, as Spirit, God seeks to evoke man's response rather than override his freedom. This does not involve any loss of human individuality, nor does it deny the historically and culturally conditioned nature of the particular human life. It is right to conclude therefore that Spirit christology does not damage the humanity of Jesus.[33]

Where the divinity is concerned, it must be remembered that early Spirit christology was not thought to be in opposition to the growing assertion of divinity. On the contrary, in some ways Spirit christology provided the root for that development. An important aspect of the Spirit christology in the New Testament is what has been termed 'double assessment', that is, 'according to the flesh' and 'according to the Spirit'. This double assessment is a root of later two-nature thought. As it was worked out, however, Spirit christology became an expression of the view that Jesus was not a divine person but a man filled with the Spirit. As such it failed to express the full force of two-nature christology and trinitarian thought. But it is possible again today to see Spirit christology not as an attack on the divinity of Christ but rather as a complement to the classical model. For it is not necessarily, as we have seen, less concerned than the two-nature model to preserve the divinity of Christ. Rather does it seek another way of expressing the vitality of that divinity, a way which does not damage his humanity. This is true, however, only when Spirit christology is part of a Spirit theology.

Spirit christology also presents an alternative way of expressing the relationship between the humanity and divinity of Jesus Christ. The most difficult problem for a Logos christology is to describe the relation of the Logos to the human soul of Jesus. Spirit christology expresses this in terms of the relation of God's Spirit to the human spirit, arguing not only that it is the Spirit of God which makes Jesus divine but also that the Spirit is the point of unity between the two natures.[34] This may appear to be a more attractive expression, simply because of the more dynamic nature of the concept. But it does depend on a fuller philosophical account of the meaning of 'spirit' than has yet been suggested, so that it may become clear whether the concept of spirit provides a natural point of unity between the divine and the human. Again, this would involve understanding God himself in terms of Spirit. For without such a doctrine of God, Spirit christology becomes a vehicle for adoptionism and its theology becomes unitarian.

These considerations of process and Spirit christologies have pointed to certain important features of a dynamic approach. We have noted, for instance, their assertion of a clear relationship between creation and christology, explicit in process theology and implicit in Spirit theology. Important though personal categories are, christology should not be limited to such categories if the redemption of creation is a serious claim. Nor, however, on the other hand, should the personal categories be lost, as perhaps they could more easily be in process thought than in Spirit christology. We have seen, too, that it is possible either to view process and Spirit christologies as straight alternatives to the classical nature model, or to see them as models to be used alongside others in a complementary fashion. It would be sensible to view them in the former way only if they were clearly able to deal more effectively than Nicaea and Chalcedon with the traditional problems of christology. Because, on the whole, as we have seen, this is not the case, their value lies in their use alongside a variety of other models, each of which seeks to state a balanced judgment about what are traditionally called the humanity and divinity of Jesus. For in the end this is the basis on which each model will rightly be judged.

Conclusion

I opened this study of contemporary trends by referring to Schleier-macher, Hegel and Ritschl, each of whom influenced one or more of the trends we have been examining. Ritschl rejects orthodox christology because it is not sufficiently influenced by what the Gospels themselves indicate about Jesus. This emphasis on the Gospels and the need for christology to begin there lies behind much of the contemporary emphasis on the humanity of Jesus and the need to do christology from below. Ritschl's influence on English thought comes largely through the writings of Herrmann, who stresses the importance of Jesus, not as belonging to the past, but as belonging to the present, thus seeking to make faith independent of the results of historical investigation.[1] This is a blend still found in modern christology: an assertion of the real humanity of Jesus, but a scepticism about the historical reliability of the gospels. Schleiermacher's influence is seen from the writings of Kähler to the work of the myth school today. His stringent criticisms of the language of the classical model have led in many cases to a rejection of the incarnation. Hegel's influence on the history of Christian doctrine is most clearly evident in those dynamic re-statements we have noted. Yet criticism of Hegel's christology as being a truth of the human race rather than of Jesus Christ is still a pertinent point to be answered by much process christology today.[2]

Contemporary theology has not therefore advanced any fundamentally new approach to christology, and the problems that we find occupying modern christology, to which I shall turn in Part Two of this book, are essentially the same as those that were beginning to be faced afresh in the nineteenth century.

PART TWO

Some Problems in Contemporary Christology

Introduction

The problems encountered in contemporary expressions of christology do not arise as a result of new attempts to restate christology. They are the same problems that christology has always confronted. Within contemporary re-expressions, however, some of the traditional problems assume a more prominent place, and it is with these in particular that we are concerned. I have selected three chief problems – the use of scripture, the historical Jesus and the uniqueness of Jesus Christ – because these are the particular problems I have encountered. It would be wrong to dismiss contemporary christology because it has failed to provide completely satisfactory solutions to these problems. This has always been the case; if it were not, Christian thought would have become more rather than less satisfied with earlier answers. We shall examine the treatment of these three areas so that we may both be able more realistically to assess the contribution of contemporary christology and also be in a better position to suggest, in Part Three of this book, further possible development.

— 4 —

The Use of Scripture

The relation of theology to scripture

The relation of theology to scripture is raised at every stage in this book. First, christology *from* below claims to reflect the basic thrust of the New Testament documents; second, suspicion of nature language is reinforced by its absence from the New Testament; and, third, process theology seeks to re-express the dynamics of Hebraic thinking and Spirit christology appeals to a primitive strand of New Testament thought. To some extent, therefore, each trend illustrates a general shift from the dogmatic to the biblical in modern theology.

There is general agreement that the biblical documents, and the New Testament in particular, are significant. For instance, it is necessary to take into account the beginnings of christology, located in the New Testament. It is necessary to understand the way that christological terms were initially used in order to build up a picture of their cultural history and later use; this can also be traced in the New Testament documents. It is further recognized that there should be no contradiction of the broad testimony of scripture, for it is there that the foundations of christology are to be found. All this means that the theologian has to give some account of the biblical foundations of his statements.

The problem is how to express more precisely what this relationship is. What does it mean to say that theology must be in accord with scripture? We can take as an example Moule's claim that concerning the manhood of Jesus there are three paradoxes central to the New Testament: the humiliation and exaltation of Jesus Christ; his continuity with and discontinuity from the rest of humanity; and the individuality yet exclusiveness of his person. Moule comments that 'no christological statement that bypasses these . . . is true to the New Testament ways of thinking'.[1]

Such a claim raises interesting questions. First, it is difficult to find agreement among expert students as to what are the central features of New Testament christology. For example, the models of incarnation and

35

inspiration both claim New Testament support. While diversity of interpretation remains, it is difficult to demand that certain specific features are essential. Second, the very variety of christological thought in the New Testament documents forces us to ask whether every feature is to be reflected in every christology. For example, it is clear that Lampe's Spirit christology is particularly dependent on Luke and Paul. In response, some may suggest that the New Testament documents reveal an ascending scale of christology leading to the expression of Jesus Christ as Saviour and Lord.[2] But this is to impose a tighter pattern than it is generally agreed is there, as well as a particular understanding of development within scripture. It would be wrong, therefore to use such a pattern as the basis for evaluating contemporary christology. In short, the New Testament documents do not provide the ingredients for later christological thinking in quite so straightforward a way as is sometimes suggested.[3]

Features of the New Testament material

It is right to recognize, therefore, that the chief reason for the lack of an unambiguous answer from the New Testament is the diversity of its material.[4] How should the theologian respond? The growing response today is to recognize and welcome this diversity, in contrast to a former determination to produce a coherent doctrinal synthesis out of the jostling biblical data.[5] There is a recognition, for example, that this diversity extends to those New Testament writings that come from the same hand: Paul's *kyrios* christology and Son of God christology express different though complementary ideas, neither of which should be considered in isolation from the other.[6] No single christology can be constructed out of Paul's letters, just as there is no single christology of the New Testament which can be systematized into the belief of the church. Only, then, in a context of recognizing such diversity is it proper to ask in what sense scripture is normative for our belief.

Yet within this diversity it is possible to ask if there is some grain or flavour, or even certain central features, of the New Testament material that can usefully be identified. At the most basic level, such unity within the agreed diversity is to be found in a common devotion to Jesus Christ.[7] But we may further seek to identify a flavour in the way New Testament writers express this devotion, and even certain general features; and we wish to argue that, taken together, these features reinforce a theological understanding of the function of christology.

The first such feature, while acknowledging the diversity of the material, concerns a number of related tensions which are key to our understanding of New Testament thought. We can use the language of contemporary christology to identify these tensions. The first is between event and person interpretations of Christ, interpretations which we shall note particularly in the later discussion of uniqueness. The second is the tension between functional and ontological interpretations. It is no longer possible to argue convincingly that the christology of the New Testament is purely functional, for the functional affirmations of early christology inevitably led to ontic affirmations.[8] The New Testament documents contain both functional and ontological categories alongside each other. The third tension is between approaches from below and from above. Contemporary christology has created a stark contrast between the two. But if we follow the grain of the New Testament, this is a false alternative.[9] For although the two distinctive approaches are to be found in the New Testament, they are not set over and against each other there.

These three pairs of tensions are aspects of a central tension between non-incarnational and incarnational interpretations of the thought of the New Testament. Their presence creates a certain amount of difficulty in many christological attempts today. But it is not so clear that it did in the minds of New Testament authors. Hebrews, for example, talks of both adoption and pre-existence with no embarrassment, and John's Gospel says both that 'I and the Father are one' (10.30) and that 'he who believes in me does not believe in me but in him who sent me' (12.44). Such tensions need to be preserved (though not exaggerated), for they belong to the very fabric of New Testament thought about Jesus.

A second feature is the apologetic character of much New Testament writing. Schillebeeckx identifies an important note when he speaks of the changing structure that characterizes the 'naming' of Jesus. It is a structure, he argues, that changes in the light of the continually shifting experience of God's gift of salvation in Jesus. It is in full accord with the New Testament, therefore, for us to give new names to Jesus, for we have a similar experience of salvation. Such new names must, however, be judged by the yardstick of their conformity to the historical reality of Jesus himself.[10] This approach is reinforced by the reminder that the New Testament came into existence in an age of conflict and by way of answer to apologetic demands. We betray the spirit of the New Testament, therefore, when we cling persistently to traditional forms even when they have ceased to convey a living and intelligible message,[11] and we reflect the New Testament when we continue to wrestle with the problem of expressing intelligently in our own environment what it means to have faith in Jesus Christ.[12]

We would do well, therefore, to accept both the apologetic character of New Testament thought and our apologetic task today, but only with some qualification. To adopt an apologetic approach in response to the approach of the New Testament does not mean that we are simply to reflect the spirit of the age. For the New Testament documents claim much that goes against the presuppositions of their own age. It is the task of the apologist, therefore, both to stand against the spirit of the age where necessary[13] and to express the gospel in terms that can be understood and believed. This is the double perspective attempted in this book, seen for example in a recognition of the significance of the contemporary stress on the humanity of Jesus on the one hand and in an assertion of the importance of belief in God rather than just interest in the figure of Jesus on the other hand. (These two aspects will lead us to seek a positive understanding of both the historical Jesus and the uniqueness of Jesus Christ.) For to fail to assert the theological implications of belief in Jesus is to abandon not only the 'substance of the tradition' but also a positive response to man's real contemporary need.

A third feature to be identified is the eschatological framework within which the christological statements of the New Testament are made.[14] The first interpreters of Jesus expressed their convictions through the use of categories with which they were familiar. This cultural conditioning does not invalidate the christological thought expressed. Rather does it suggest the importance of the early belief that Jesus, as the eschatological figure, came from God and after his death was vindicated by God. Much modern christology from below suggests that the Fathers imposed an approach from above on the primitive pattern found in the New Testament. But the thoroughly eschatological character of the New Testament documents reminds us that the primitive earliest approach was not just from below. Its eschatological dimension prevents that simple conclusion.[15]

This is not to argue that an eschatological approach leads directly and unequivocally to the doctrine of the incarnation, but rather to see it as one approach to such a theology. For the eschatology of the New Testament involves an assertion of the ultimate significance of the life, death and resurrection of Jesus Christ[16] and is therefore seen as an invitation to define the ultimate meaning and purpose of human life by reference to Jesus Christ as a life which embodies the definitive activity of God himself.[17] Non-incarnational christology finds it difficult to express this ultimacy; indeed, it is adopted by many precisely because it does not entail this. Yet the eschatology found in the New Testament expresses this note persistently, either by implication or explicitly. Incarnational thought is one clear way of reflecting it.[18]

The eschatological nature of New Testament christology is, however, a reminder that all christological talk is provisional in character. Our knowledge of God is as yet provisional and our statements about God in Christ are therefore also provisional.[19] Final knowledge of God belongs to the eschaton. This would seem to underline the need for a plurality of models, such as we do in fact find in the New Testament. For the use of a plurality of models indicated their provisional character, without however challenging the ultimacy of God in Jesus Christ. It is therefore the eschatological nature of New Testament statements about Christ which indicates that they are intended to point to the mystery of God. In the same way, the eschatological nature of christology today reminds us that christology is a servant of theology, for the significance of Jesus Christ is to do with the relation in which he stands to God.

The relation of these factors to christology

I have tried to identify in general terms three features of New Testament thought: tensions, apologetic and eschatology. Now we must ask what use the systematic theologian should make of them. Unlike those noted by Moule, these features are less particularly features of the person of Christ and more generally refer to the outlook, approach and mood of the New Testament. I suggest that they should be taken into account by every christology which seeks to be related to the original documents in a way that invites the New Testament to act as some sort of correction or even norm. This is necessary because theology is all one and cannot be divided into separate parts, biblical and systematic. A synthesis must therefore continually be sought,[20] not for the purpose of reflecting the thought of selected biblical passages, but so that christology may be influenced by the central perspective of the New Testament. How is this to be worked out?

Some recent studies have debated whether the relationship between the New Testament and later christology is better expressed in terms of development or evolution.[21] The evolutionary model suggests that the genesis of christology can be explained in the manner of the history-of-religions school of thought, that is, that the characteristics of Christ in the New Testament arose out of contact with extraneous sources. The development models speak of growth from immaturity to maturity and of the characteristics of Christ in the New Testament springing from contact with Jesus himself. According to this view, the various estimates of Christ are attempts to describe what was already there from the beginning. To affirm that all development is of this kind and that none, in principle, is caused by 'outside' influence appears to be a rejection of the possibility of God being at work outside the person of Christ and a rejection of the apologetic nature of Christian theology. Moreover, in practice it is often difficult to make a clear distinction between evolution and development, between outside influences and what can be perceived to have been present in principle in Jesus Christ from the beginning. The two models need not therefore be deemed mutually exclusive.[22]

Far more important, however, than whether development or evolution is the more correct model is the question of what is to be judged as right development, and on what grounds.[23] For this is the substance of the argument between evolution and development: were the changes that took place, both within the New Testament and later, right steps or not? How is it possible to judge whether change has been in the right direction, and does the New Testament play any role in this assessment?

One possible approach is through the use of the model of translation. For example, it is asked whether the statement 'Jesus is God incarnate' is a correct or possible translation of what the New Testament says, or a mistranslation.[24] The model does, however, present some difficulty, for it appears to suggest that there is a single agreed original New Testament christology which can be consulted in order to verify a contemporary expression and which can be translated in each age. We have seen that the New Testament does not provide precisely this; though some would argue that it does provide a foundation datum or norm for christology which can be used in this way.[25] Refinements of, or alternatives to, the translation model (such as redescription, change through the alteration of perspective, rediscovery by each generation of Jesus Christ for itself)[26] share the same basic feature. Each expresses the need for the contemporary expression to be checked, corrected or balanced by what is said in the New Testament. This is why I have identified in outline what some of those basic features or characteristics are.

I believe that such an identification is essential if theology is to be related properly to scripture. It is necessary if, for example, we speak of a continuity of basic aims or intentions.[27] Attractive though this may seem, aims and intentions are difficult to be sure about, as they involve a calculated guess as to motive. We are on firmer ground if we simply seek to reflect the perspective and central thrust of the New Testament documents along the lines I have indicated. Then it is possible to avoid the alleged 'protestant' selection and distortion of texts, associated with the view that scripture alone is sufficient, and the alleged 'catholic' false exegesis, associated with the view that theology must not contradict scripture but must be shown to be present there in embryo. For the New Testament must be allowed to question and challenge our christological thinking, so that the person of Jesus Christ, as he is found in scripture, may question and challenge our presuppositions about God. This in the end is the function of christology, but it is able to fulfil it properly only if it is dynamically related to the New Testament confessions about Jesus Christ. We shall explore this in Part Three where I shall offer some examples of the effect of this understanding of the function of christology.

A reflection on the historical influence of the New Testament

It still remains to enquire how far in practice the New Testament was used in the formulation of christology within the early church. It is clear that, to begin with, Jewish scripture provided the basic source documents for christological reflection, for it was not until the third century that a clear notion of New Testament canon emerged. The interpretation of Jewish scripture was of course determined by the central conviction about Jesus Christ. Paul, Matthew's Gospel and Justin Martyr all used belief in Christ as their basic hermeneutical principle. Nevertheless Jewish scripture played an enormous role in formulating and supporting early doctrine. The early Fathers were exegetes, and it was Jewish scripture that they were interpreting. The two processes of the development of doctrine and the definition of certain Christian writings as scripture went on, therefore, simultaneously.

Nor is it clear that the New Testament canon, when defined, began to have greater influence in the continuing development of doctrine. It was simply presumed that the Old Testament and the New Testament confirmed each other, and the newness of the New Testament was obscured. Thus the Old Testament continued to provide christological texts even after the New Testament had emerged.[28] Later, it is true, appeal to the Old Testament was replaced; but usually it was replaced by appeal to the Fathers, who themselves had appealed to Jewish scripture. Gradually this appeal to the Fathers became of greater importance, and collections of patristic texts replaced collections of Old Testament texts. An appeal to scripture became in effect an appeal to the correct interpretation of scripture. When the New Testament was used, it was to support an interpretation already largely determined.[29]

41

If this general reconstruction is basically correct, it would appear that the New Testament documents have not yet been allowed sufficiently to influence our christology, and through our christology our understanding of God. This is why the question of the relation of contemporary christology to scripture is so important.

Assessment

It does not follow from this, however, that every contemporary christological presentation which claims New Testament support is to be preferred to the traditional statements of Nicaea and Chalcedon. It means rather that both traditional and modern christologies are to be evaluated and corrected according to our understanding of New Testament thought.

Such evaluation involves taking account of a number of specific factors. First, it involves a recognition of the variety of approach found in the New Testament. This alone can encourage the renewal of christology today. It also suggests that no one single model will be found adequate but that each will need the complement of others. Second, it involves recognizing that underlying the variety of approach there is the historical figure of Jesus of Nazareth. For, despite their different approaches, the New Testament writers never give up their identification of the exalted Christ with the historical figure. Each christology, functional, mythological or ontological, is grounded in Jesus of Nazareth. Third, it involves reflecting those features of the New Testament approach to christology that I have suggested make up its grain or flavour. Modern christology need not be afraid of reflecting the tension found in the New Testament, and it must strive to preserve both the apologetic and the eschatological dimension. Fourth, it involves an acceptance that the basic context in which christology is developed is a theological one. It is a dangerous half-truth to suggest that the New Testament is totally christocentric,[30] for Jesus-talk does not replace God-talk. Rather is the context of christology ('Jesus-talk') always a desire for a deeper knowledge of God. 'Jesus stands for God' in the important sense that the New Testament writers describe God through their descriptions of Jesus Christ, and experience the presence of God through their experience of the risen Christ. This means that what is most important in the New Testament is not what it says about Jesus Christ, but what it is saying about God. For Christian experience of Christ – in his ministry, death and resurrection – has led to a new understanding of God, his character and our beliefs about him. It is these things which Christian thought has yet fully to work out and express theologically.

— 5 —

The Historical Jesus

The issue raised

The issue of the historical Jesus has been raised at many points in this essay. In particular, the discussion of the tendency to stress the humanity of Jesus led us to ask whether the insistence on preserving the ordinary humanity of Jesus was an expression of a principle or a matter which could be evidenced and supported by historical investigation. At its best, christology from below is not the mere assertion of something in principle, but is concerned to assert that the historical event has actually taken place. The starting point of such christology, if it is to be convincing, must therefore be the historical concreteness of the event.[1] If the criticism of later incarnational theology is that it concentrated on the finished incarnation in a way which prevented a proper recognition of the ordinary humanity of Jesus, any corrective to this cannot be satisfied with an assertion of the reality of such humanity. It must rather be prepared to begin again with the historical Jesus and trace the steps through for itself.

It has been claimed that if there is one point upon which almost all contemporary Christian theologians are agreed, it is the utter reality of the manhood of Jesus Christ.[2] But unfortunately there is no agreement on what precisely this alleged 'real' humanity is rooted in and evidenced by – his limitation of knowledge, his freedom, or what.[3] In other words, it is easier to assert such a claim in principle than to assert its particularity. This illustrates with what care we must approach the issue of the historical Jesus.

The sinlessness of Jesus

The question of the sinlessness of Jesus has become a focus for the wider question of the nature of his humanity.[4] For to claim sinlessness for Jesus is one possible way of affirming the nature of his humanity. 'Real' humanity is usually associated with the condition of sin. But is such a supposition correct? Chalcedon claims the uniqueness not only of the divinity of Jesus Christ but also of his humanity. This claim is usually taken to involve his sinlessness. Does such sinlessness separate his humanity from ours?

Such questioning raises the issue of our understanding of sin. In common usage, sin is given an entirely negative meaning. But there is some advantage in speaking in more positive terms of the human goodness of Jesus. Certainly process theology encourages such a perspective and therefore speaks of sin as a deviation of aim, on the grounds that man is made for love.[5] Byzantine theology also stresses that man is made in the image of the transcendent God: his very nature allows man to go beyond himself and communicate with his archetype.[6] Such approaches do not see divinization as the abolition of a truly human nature, but as the fulfilment of what it means to be human. This provides a framework in which it may be possible to affirm the sinlessness of Jesus in terms of his positive fulfilment of humanity rather than as a denial of his real humanity.

There still remains, however, the question of the grounds on which an assertion of sinlessness is to be made. There appears to be three possibilities, namely, historical investigation, New Testament witness, theological assertion.

Concerning historical investigation, it can safely be affirmed that there really is no possibility of coming to such a conclusion. There is simply not the evidence available – neither a list of sins Jesus did not commit, nor a description of his human goodness in such detail that would enable the historian to draw the probable conclusion of his sinlessness.[7] 'Event christology' has to face this problem more acutely than 'person christology,'[8] for person christology is not caught up as directly in the same sort of difficult historical questions. Event christology must always submit itself to historical judgments, even though, as in this case, there is insufficient evidence. The lack of evidence is partly because of the nature of the sources (the Gospels are of a theological nature and give scant historical detail), and partly because there never could be sufficient historical detail to affirm without doubt the sinlessness, in thought, word and deed, of any particular human life. Historical investigation could, however, deny such a claim.

Concerning the witness of the New Testament documents, the evidence to be found there has to be interpreted, and thus theological judgments are inevitably brought to bear on the material. For example, when Pannenberg argues that we must not work from the claim that Jesus did not commit sin to a claim about his unity with God, but rather from the resurrection as an affirmation of his unity with God to the conclusion that Jesus was without sin, he is making a claim based on his own theological judgment.[9] Others would interpret the same documents differently. There is therefore no simple, straightforward, unambiguous and agreed way in which the sinlessness of Jesus can be derived from the New Testament documents.

It becomes clear, therefore, that it is only on the basis of a theological judgment, a judgment about both human nature in general and the person of Christ in particular, that the sinlessness of Christ can be cogently affirmed. A belief in the incarnation provides such a basis, and it is not easy to know on what basis the sinlessness of Jesus can be affirmed in those theologies which dismiss the incarnational approach altogether.[10] A person christology does not rely on historical investigation to establish its claim. Its basis is theological, namely, an affirmation of Christ's unity with God. Sinlessness then becomes Christ's uninterrupted unity with God. But the claim to this unity, unbroken by sin, is not positively founded on historical or biblical investigation, though it may be supported in the sense that the historical and biblical material does not contradict it. This brief discussion of the sinlessness of Jesus serves therefore to raise the important question of the role of historical investigation in the Christian assessment of the person of Jesus Christ.

The quest

The old quest for the historical Jesus failed for a number of reasons. It became a blind alley, producing fluctuating biographies which had no inherent power to convince of their authenticity but rather served to conceal the living Christ.[11] A review of these lives of Jesus shows not only their wide divergencies but also the close resemblance between a particular writer's picture of Jesus and his general view on social and religious questions.[12] What therefore was produced was only a reflection of a liberal protestant face seen at the bottom of a deep well.[13] These judgments were all made on the particular results of nineteenth-century investigations. Behind such criticisms lies Lessing's more fundamental claim not only that there is insufficient historical justification for the claims of the Christian faith, but also that truth cannot be substantiated by historical means nor imparted in an historical way.[14]

Despite such judgments, a new quest of the historical Jesus has emerged. Its aim, however, is not a return to the old quest nor an avoidance of the commitment to faith. Rather does it seek to enquire into the significance of the historical Jesus for faith: to find out what his preaching

was and to establish a link between the exalted and the earthly Jesus.[15]
The new quest has not, however, escaped criticism and much of that
criticism is very similar to that directed against the old quest: a false confidence is restored in the capacity of the historian to tell us the ultimate
truth about Jesus Christ;[16] the presentation of Jesus is of a suspiciously
modern figure, one who lacks a first-century dimension;[17] there is no
picture of the historical Jesus behind the biblical picture which could be
made scientifically probable, and therefore the new quest has brought no
change for the systematic theologian.[18]

It is important to be clear what is the basic criticism of the new quest
that lies behind such comments. It is not that the new quest seeks to
establish continuity between Jesus and the kerygma. Such personal continuity is accepted.[19] The issue concerns the basis of such continuity. For
the new quest, like the old, gives a prominent role to historical investigation in asserting this continuity. Its opponents claim that only faith can
provide the basis for continuity. Tillich, for example, on the one hand
rejects the old and the new quest, and on the other hand discusses the
details of the words, deeds and suffering of Jesus, as though he were talking about the historical Jesus. In fact, he is talking about the biblical
picture of Jesus. For him, it is faith, not historical investigation, which
guarantees that the concrete biblical picture is an adequate expression of
the New Being in Jesus as the Christ.[20] He has assigned to faith the role
that others have assigned to historical investigation.

The role of historical investigation

Is there any role left for historical investigation, and, if so, what is its
purpose in christological study? We wish to argue that there is need for a
modified reliance on the support that historical investigation can give to
christology.

First, the assertion of the humanity of Jesus, so central to most contemporary thought, becomes not only a bare but an empty principle unless
something can be asserted with reasonable probability about the historical
figure.[21] The argument that historical investigation can lead only to
probabilities and can never give absolute certainty is accepted, but it is
no more relevant to the study of Jesus of Nazareth than to a study of any
other figure of history – unless more is being claimed for the historical
picture than such investigation will support.

Second, it is important to illustrate that Christianity did begin with
Jesus.[22] He was the central figure around whom the Christian faith began.
His life, death and resurrection are the vital factors which led to the

various New Testament documents. Though a detailed biography is neither possible nor necessary, it is essential that some substance be given to this central figure. A portrait has to be built up to ensure that there is no contradiction between the sort of person he was and the truths about him inherent in what Christianity claims.

Third, without such historical investigation Jesus easily becomes a figure to be manipulated by Christians who wish to root their interpretation of the faith in the life of Jesus.[23] Ironically, this is precisely what happened with those nineteenth-century attempts to write his life. But it is vital that our understanding of the Christian life be corrected by what we can discover about what Jesus was like and who he was.

For these reasons I argue that a primary task of Christian theology is to build up what picture it can of Jesus of Nazareth using the best critical scholarship and all the tools of historical investigation. It is right to ask, however, whether such historical-critical scholarship can provide sufficient knowledge about this figure of history for the systematic theologian to build christologically on this foundation. 'Sufficient for what?' is the key question. The purpose of such historical investigation is not to write a biography; it is rather to root our christological interpretation in the earthly life of a real person. Without this, the kerygma becomes separated from his earthly life in a way which cuts Christian theology off from its historical roots and so deprives it of its life. This is because the truth of a christological statement is dependent upon the truth of a historical statement about Jesus, at least to the extent that historical investigation does not contradict, but rather supports, the christological claim. We need therefore constantly to refer to the historical Jesus as the norm of christological judgments.[24]

From this there follows a more significant purpose of historical investigation. For just as christological reflection is dependent on historical investigation, so christology is not an end in itself but leads on to theology. For the purpose of christology is to be a servant of theology. In the end, therefore, our understanding of God is dependent on historical investigation in the sense that historical investigation supports or corrects, confirms or denies christological judgments, judgments which in the end affect our understanding of God. For example, our present understanding of God as a loving father is dependent both on our understanding of Christ's relationship with God and on his teaching about and experience of God. This is the proper pattern of theology: historical study, christology, theology.

The most important reason, therefore, why it is important to discover what we can about the historical figure of Jesus is that we wish to build up a picture of his theological qualities. By 'theological qualities' is meant his relationship with God, his understanding of God, his teaching about God. Although these cannot be separated from his human characteristics, but rather are expressed in them, it is these theological qualities on which we need to focus through historical investigation.[25] It is important that theological claims are not made which cannot be supported in this way, and that theological claims about Jesus are not made in terms which suggest that they can be supported by historical investigation, if this is not the case.[26] Nevertheless, Jesus' own understanding of God is of fundamental importance, and the documents which relate to this need to be historically investigated. For Jesus' own experience of God is a foundation of the disciples' experience of God. Their experience was made possible by Jesus and their experience reflects his, as the *abba* passages illustrate.

The relation between faith and history

Let us summarize, therefore, the practical relationship between faith and history. First, if historical investigation suggests that Jesus was something quite different from what faith affirms, the kerygmatic faith has become untenable. So historical investigation – biblical research – has the role of testing the continuity between Jesus of Nazareth and the preached Christ. The New Testament knows no chasm here. The blending of history and theology is an integral part of Christianity, and is found in the literary form of the gospels where kerygmatic claims are made in the context of the story of Jesus. Early Christian traditions, too, are more or less both reflections about Jesus of Nazareth and kerygmatic confessions. The two cannot convincingly be divided,[27] and christology today cannot sustain a radical breach between what we know by faith and what we know through historical investigation.

Second, the role of historical investigation is to confirm faith where it can, to support faith from its study of the figure of Jesus, and to correct and if necessary deny christological faith not confirmed by the evidence. Historical investigation cannot create faith, and it must not seek to extend its role in this respect. It cannot demonstrate on its own that God is involved in a quite special way in the person of Jesus Christ. This is the decision of faith. Historical investigation cannot turn the words and works of Jesus into christology, for christology is a faith-judgment about Jesus. But it is a faith-judgment not ruled out by the conclusions of critical study. If this were not so, christology would be free to allow any statement about man's salvation to be treated as Christian, precisely because the test of the historical root would remain unconsidered.[28] The support that faith and historical study give is mutual: for just as historical investigation cannot create faith, faith cannot create the Jesus event – it is dependent on it. There is no kerygma apart from Jesus of Nazareth.

Third, there is a certain risk in accepting the mutual supporting roles of faith and history. This is because historical investigation cannot produce certainty. This does not mean, however, that faith should avoid being based on historical judgments, in order to preserve its certainty. It is indeed a false dilemma to suggest that we must either confirm beyond doubt by historical methods that the historical Jesus will carry the weight of Christian theology, or do theology without regard to historical investigation.[29] Faith involves risk. Its risk may be primarily existential, but there is no good reason to exclude the risk of history from the risk of faith.[30] While it would be wrong to exaggerate the risk,[31] the risk cannot be eliminated, and faith has to accept it.

Assessment

The term 'the historical Jesus' is used in a variety of ways. It is used to describe the results of historical investigation, to describe the product of scriptural exegesis, to describe the results of the study of extra-biblical material. The term is also used to affirm that there was an historical figure, but that no details can, or need be, discovered about him, or that there is no one historical Jesus but only the relative standpoints of Matthew, Mark, Luke and John.[32] This wide variety of understanding, interpretation and use of the term suggests the need for some clarification.

The clarification of the term is related to the understanding of history. For Bultmann's view of history as an encounter with the past has helped to diminish the importance of discovering what can be known by strictly historical methods. Significant though an existentialist interpretation of history may be, it is of first importance to discover the actual event upon which any interpretation may be based. I support, therefore, the suggestion that the term 'historical Jesus' should be used of 'Jesus, in so far as he can be made the object of critical historical research'.[33]

This battle to preserve the decisive element of historical reality is not a new one arising simply out of an existential understanding of history. It is a battle fought previously. For example, the framework of Platonic Hermetic doctrine seemed to many at the time to be so near to the Christian belief in revelation that it was questionable whether it was necessary to become Christian at all. But the Hermetic theory lacked this decisive element of historical reality: it spoke of human lostness and of man's destiny, but it did not root this theory in a historical life.[34] This mistake is never found in the New Testament documents, varied though their treatment of the historical figure is.

My conclusion, therefore, is that the study of the historical figure is necessary as a base for christology, without which there is no adequate foundation for moving forward to Christian theology. For, in the end, the study of the historical figure is significant because of the claim that God himself is disclosed in and through him. Setting it in this theological context prevents the study of the historical figure leading to jesuology, in which the human Jesus is the object of faith. But there can be no christology without him at its centre, for this would be to make christology a mere ideology.[35] Jesuology was thrust into becoming christology because Jesus could not be contained within the religious categories of his day. Christology too needs to move beyond itself, as jesuology did. Christology becomes a theological subject when it is recognized that the most important feature of the historical Jesus is his relation to and with God. For christology's proper role is a theological one: it points us to God; but its root is historical: it points us back to Jesus of Nazareth in whom God was present and active.

The Uniqueness of Jesus Christ

The question is raised

We have seen that the question of the uniqueness of Jesus Christ is raised by all three trends in contemporary thought. First, an emphasis on the humanity of Jesus is christologically inadequate unless it is accompanied by a recognition of his special relationship with God. Without this there is no adequate reason for Christian theology to be preoccupied with Jesus of Nazareth. Second, a rejection of the traditional two-nature model involves the rejection of one clear way of asserting uniqueness, namely, a metaphysical uniqueness of the eternal Son made man at the incarnation (though process theology suggests another way of asserting metaphysical uniqueness). Third, dynamic models have raised the question of whether Jesus is one who simply emerged from a series and is therefore in principle no different from any other emergent being, or whether there is a break in the emerging series which accounts for the uniqueness of Christ. Likewise, Spirit christology has to face the question of how Jesus is to be distinguished from other inspired people.

The question of uniqueness is also raised by the phenomenon of other world religions. Contact with other faiths has led to a questioning of the claim that Christianity is unique and this in turn has raised the question of the uniqueness of Jesus Christ. For although these are two different questions, they bear a close relationship. The uniqueness of Christianity would probably depend on the uniqueness of Jesus Christ, but an assertion of the uniqueness of Jesus Christ does not necessarily lead to any claim about the Christian religion. Dialogue between world religions involves self-judgment and an association with other quests for truth. In this context it is possible to argue that Jesus Christ is the criterion by which all religion should be judged, including Christianity.[1] Clearly there is need for any general christological approach to be compatible with the attitude taken to religious pluralism, if contradiction is to be avoided.[2] Here a theological understanding of christology helps, for the pheno-

menon of world religions indicates that God is the source of salvation and
suggests that different religions are different responses to God's self-
revelation.[3] For the Christian, God's presence and activity in Jesus Christ
remains the decisive indication of what he is like, but this does not rule
out the contributions of other religions.

The hypothetical existence of intelligent life on other planets raises the
same question as religious pluralism, though in a different form. Here the
question is whether Christ is to be restricted to historical mankind and
whether there are other ways of divine self-manifestation more appropriate to other worlds. One way to accommodate this possibility is to
speak of the universal character of the Logos who was experienced in
Jesus Christ in a unique way for historical mankind and who may be
expressed in other ways for other parts of creation.[4] A simpler way, however, is to ground all such revelation in God himself, as with other religions. There is no need to invoke the symbol of the universal Logos to
cope with either other religions or other planets; the notion of the universal God is quite adequate.

Chalcedon's adequacy?

Now that we have noted the form in which contemporary christology
raises the question of uniqueness, we must ask how the traditional expression of that claim, as found in the Chalcedonian formula, measures up to
the way the question presents itself today. We note, however, that a
cause of the failure of many alternative christologies to have been more
than a passing alternative has been their inadequate treatment of the
radical distinctiveness of Christ.[5] Our question, therefore, is not confined to Chalcedon's ability to meet contemporary needs; it concerns,
too, the ability of non-incarnational christologies to express a proper
distinctiveness.

In the light of other religions and the possibility of intelligent life on
other planets, we must enquire of the Chalcedonian understanding of the
uniqueness of Christ whether it denies the presence of God apart from
his presence in Jesus Christ. Does Chalcedon's claim to uniqueness,
embedded as it is in an incarnational framework, mean that God was
present in Jesus Christ in a way he was not present anywhere else? The
issue of suffering can be used to illustrate the question: was God present
in the suffering of Jesus Christ in a way he is not present in other suffering? A claim to the uniqueness of Jesus Christ does not in fact require
such a view. On the contrary, an incarnational approach may be taken to
indicate that presence in all suffering rather than prevent it.[6] For an

affirmation of God's unique personal presence in the cross does not make him less present in the suffering of humanity, but rather does his own suffering in Christ affirm that he is present in humanity's suffering. If the incarnation is understood in this way, it is not seen as a limitation, but as an indication, of God's presence. This debate, however, does show that the uniqueness of Christ cannot be treated merely as a christological question, but quickly becomes a theological one, that is, one about God's presence.

If, however, the incarnation is treated in this way (as indicative of God's universal presence), does it demand a confession of the uniqueness of Jesus Christ? The phenomenon of other religions and the presence of other planets both suggest the possibility that God could have revealed himself in other lives, for the sake of sections of mankind outside the Judaeo-Christian tradition and for the sake of other intelligent life-forms. In this case, the incarnation would not be unique; there would be revelations other than in Jesus Christ.[7] In classical christology, the term 'incarnation' is used in a more limited way to describe the personal presence of the eternal Son of God. To use it of other religious figures (such as Elijah and Gandhi) is to extend its use from the traditional 'once for all' meaning. To use it to describe a general feature of human life would be to extend its use even further, and to begin to abandon the model of incarnation for that of adoption – in which case the concept of uniqueness has been more or less abandoned too.[8] It would seem, therefore, that either we should retain a more limited use of the term incarnation and its associated claim to uniqueness, or abandon the language of incarnation and with it any clear implication of uniqueness. This is not to argue, however, that Chalcedon's understanding of the uniqueness of Christ necessarily rules out the one, unique God's expression of himself in a whole number of different ways, both in other religions and on other planets.

Difference in kind or in degree

The matter, however, is complicated by the fact that the concept of uniqueness is understood in different ways. One common distinction is between a difference in kind and a difference in degree. The concept of a difference in degree arises out of a desire not to exaggerate the difference between Jesus and the rest of mankind, and is seen, for example, in the desire of process christology not to postulate a break in the chain. It is also found in the desire to treat Jesus Christ as a genuine sample of the whole, a typical representative of humanity, who, through his own resurrection, becomes the leading shoot of a new spiritual humanity.[9] In a similar way, it is argued that in Jesus Christ there has been an immeasurably greater realization of potentiality but not something utterly removed from the experience of mankind elsewhere: he is unique in fact but not in principle.[10] The principal purpose therefore of this distinction between 'in kind' and 'in degree' is to preserve the real humanity of Jesus of Nazareth.[11]

The treatment of a merely human figure as the object of devotion is the most serious danger inherent in degree christology. For degree christology suggests that his difference from other men is a difference in degree of some human possibility such as faith, obedience to God, openness to God, or authority. Such claims could be established only by historical investigation, and, as we have seen, while historical investigation may support our beliefs about Jesus Christ, it is not able satisfactorily to establish any claim to the uniqueness of a particular human characteristic of Jesus. More seriously still, such an objective is a return to jesuology, a return to the devotion of some human characteristic. Such a neo-Arian approach fails to express the basic theological dimension of christology. For if there is no real difference between the humanity of Jesus and ordinary humanity, the person of Christ cannot bear the weight of christology;[12] and if Jesus did not have so special a relationship to, and with, God (such as is not expressed in a degree christology), christology cannot fulfil its theological role.[13]

We have seen that one attempt to preserve the Chalcedonian emphasis and at the same time to do justice to the contemporary concern with the humanity of Jesus is to speak in terms of human transcendence.[14] This argues that Jesus transcends humanity and his uniqueness lies in his being man, for being man was the form of God's revelation. His divinity is known from the manner in which he is human, for he is human in a completely unique way: in Jesus Christ, God declares what it is to be human. Such an approach provides a context in which it becomes possible to think of humanity and divinity being united in a single person, in the way Chalcedon suggests, while not being confined to the philosophical framework in which Chalcedon was conceived and expressed. Nevertheless, it is clear that in such a notion of human transcendence the humanity of Jesus is not confined to our humanity and the demand that his humanity be conceived as merely ordinary is not met. This is inevitable, for in no other way is it possible for us to move beyond observations about a historical figure to the beginnings of christology. Unless it be allowed that in some way God was specially, uniquely 'present' and 'active' in Jesus Christ, christology is still-born.[15]

Exclusive or inclusive uniqueness

A further distinction is made between exclusive and inclusive uniqueness. An exclusive understanding of uniqueness involves a denial of God's revelation in and through others, such as we have discussed in terms of other religions and other intelligent life. It is this implication which causes many who wish to accept the possibility of God's revelation elsewhere to reject a claim to uniqueness altogether on the grounds of the intolerance and exclusive-minded attitude it produces.[16] For it is argued that to assert that, as the unique Son of God, Jesus Christ is the one and only point of saving contact between God and man is to contradict the notion of the limitless love of God. For such a view would seem to imply that the vast majority of mankind is damned.[17] The question, therefore, is whether a claim to uniqueness does necessarily imply that God can be adequately known and responded to only through Jesus. It is clear that much contemporary christology rejects this implication, is opposed to all claims to exclusiveness for Jesus Christ or for Christianity, and seeks instead a christology which is more open and tolerant.[18]

It is equally clear that no objection is being raised in respect of claims made for the uniqueness and universality of God. The difficulties expressed concern an exclusive understanding of Christ's uniqueness. The point at issue therefore is whether this uniqueness and universality which belongs to God has been given a historically particular reference in the life of Jesus.

One way in which this may be expressed, while meeting the proper objections raised, is to speak of Christ's uniqueness in an inclusive sense. The phrase 'inclusive uniqueness' refers to a uniqueness of such a kind that it includes within it qualities found elsewhere. It is argued, for example, that in the New Testament there is a great affirmative inclusiveness in what is claimed for Jesus Christ, 'which, in principle, evidently involves all, anywhere and everywhere, that may be called the utterance – the Logos – of God'.[19] John's Gospel identifies in the man Jesus of Nazareth the eternal Logos which, it claims, enlightens every man. It is a claim that has 'an immense inclusiveness' about it, for it suggests that wherever God speaks this is embodied in the man Jesus of Nazareth. Such attempts to interpret uniqueness in an inclusive sense are attempts to assert a personal uniqueness for Jesus Christ which does not prevent God's revelation through others. The concept of inclusive uniqueness illustrates that it is only when the issue is expressed in theological rather than merely christological terms that a resolution of the question of uniqueness becomes possible.

Person or event

The possibility of a more direct theological understanding of uniqueness arises out of the further distinction between event and person christology. An event christology regards Jesus Christ as remarkable, not so much for what he was in himself as for what God has done through him.[20] It lends itself more than person christology to the belief that Jesus was different from other men only in degree. For it suggests that God was not at work in Jesus in an altogether different way from his activity in other men but rather that there was a concentration of God's activity in the event of Jesus Christ. Its advantage over other degree christology, however, is that it identifies the uniqueness in terms of God, albeit only a degree of uniqueness through God's activity. However, in event christology the special activity of God is identified in a wider context than the life of Jesus. It is associated with the total event of which Christ is seen as the focus or centre. In support of event christology, it is argued that the New Testament claims a finality for what God has done in Jesus Christ but not that the pattern of his life was unique. A person christology, on the other hand, usually asserts more than a difference in degree, claiming that the person of Christ was different in kind from other men.

There is considerable danger if event christology is associated with a marked degree of historical scepticism. For then the event, already somewhat generalized, is dissipated into a wide series of preparatory and consequential events, none of which is historically sure. When such historical scepticism is applied to the centre of these events, namely, the life, death and resurrection of Jesus Christ, it becomes difficult to know upon what precise events the christology is based.[21] It is this particular combination of historical scepticism and event christology which causes this acute problem. For how can an event christology be developed on such an unsure foundation? Unmitigated historical scepticism therefore effectively prevents any development of a plausible event christology as an alternative to person christology.

Event christology raises the question of how God acts in history, as well as the more specific question about the way he acted decisively in Jesus Christ. This is a fundamental question which affects our whole approach to christology because it is a question about the sort of God we believe in.[22] For example, a difference in understanding the alleged virginal conception of Jesus is caused by a fundamental disagreement about how God acts in the world. Does he work through natural processes or does he cut across these natural processes in what is often called miraculous activity? There is clearly a need to clarify what sort of talk it is to say that God has acted in human history before using this as a christological model. Is it, for instance, more than a way of speaking about the way man interprets his experience?[23] All talk about God is indirect or analogous; he does not act in history in the same way that men and women do, though he may act principally through people. For event christology to be of value, a way has to be discovered of speaking about God acting in history which avoids, on the one hand, a crude interventionist concept of God, such as is found in much Yahwistic history[24] and, on the other hand, the inference that it is no more than our faith-assessment of Jesus or his attitude to God.

A better analogy than 'action' is 'presence'. It suggests a more personal category.[25] It allows the possibility of using the attractive analogy of spiritual presence.[26] It is not subject to the difficulties which, we have seen, are associated with the activity of God in event christology.[27] Person christology expresses more directly the theological nature of christology through using a term which points to God's personal presence in Jesus Christ. Of course, preference for the analogy of presence does not deny God's activity in the life of Jesus. On the contrary, it suggests a way in which it can be affirmed: God was able to act personally in Jesus Christ because he was personally present.

The New Testament

There are two particular matters concerning the New Testament understanding of the person of Christ which relate to his uniqueness and concern the value of person christology in particular. They are the eschatological origin of the concept of Christ's uniqueness and the occurrence, if at all, of the concept of personal pre-existence.

The search for the origin of the uniqueness of Jesus Christ is a search for what gave rise to this reflection in the life of the early Church. The search has concentrated on the eschatological context in which Christianity was born, a context which naturally gave rise to a sense of the ultimacy of Christ's work. What is disputed is whether this ultimacy or uniqueness ascribed to Christ is comprehensible apart from the eschatological framework within which it arose. Does the discovery of its eschatological origin mean its rejection for those who hold a different world-view today?[28] The implication that because he was a product of his day, Jesus was imprisoned within its thought-forms, fails to do justice to the distinctive way in which Jesus rose above his own culture.[29] For although Jesus fulfilled the hopes of Judaism, he did so in such a way that many failed to recognize him as

Messiah. This was because he transcended their expectations, including the passing eschatological perspective of his day. Eschatology became the framework within which belief in the uniqueness of his person and the ultimacy of his work was expressed. This same belief about him continued to be expressed in a Greek framework later on, and can still be held today quite apart from the value we may choose to place on an eschatological understanding of life. The substance of this argument is that the real origin of the belief in the uniqueness of the person of Jesus Christ lies in the active presence of God in that personal life. The assertion of the eschatological origin of uniqueness does not therefore deny either the continued belief in his uniqueness or the use of person christology to express it.

The second question is also related to the difference between a person and an event christology. The question of personal pre-existence does not, of course, arise in an event christology, but is raised only in the context of person christology. Does the New Testament speak in terms of personal pre-existence? On the one hand, pre-existence can be seen as the individual personality of the historical figure retrospected on to a pre-existent heavenly person.[30] On this reading of the New Testament, the use of the language of pre-existence in Paul, Hebrews and John is not intended to identify personal pre-existence; it points at the most only to a life or power which comes to expression in an individual person. On the other hand, the presence of these same statements of personal pre-existence can be interpreted as part of the writers' belief about Jesus Christ to be placed alongside the other things they say, such as assertions of his ordinary humanity.[31] On this reading, the remarkable feature of the writings of Paul, Hebrews and John is that they assert both that Jesus was a man and that he possessed personal pre-existence in a way which suggests that they could not offer a solution to this state of affairs, nor did they see the need to do so. A belief in the personal pre-existence of Jesus Christ is there, it is argued, as an expression of their belief that the God who had revealed himself in Jesus Christ was the same God who had revealed himself to Israel. The value of this analysis is that by understanding uniqueness in terms of God the whole issue of personal pre-existence is able to be seen in theological terms: 'God as manifest in the wholly human life of Jesus is the same God who has always sought to communicate himself to men.'

Assessment

This discussion of the problem of the uniqueness of Jesus Christ does not pretend to offer a solution to the difficulties associated with it. I have indicated the chief options available to christology today and offered criticisms of these from a particular perspective. I have rejected those christologies which tend to displace God from their estimate of who Jesus is, and welcomed those which combined a recognition of contemporary concerns with a recognition that christology is chiefly concerned with expressing the Christian belief of God's 'presence' and 'activity' in Jesus Christ. This perspective arises out of the conviction, to be explored more fully in Part Three of this book, that christology is a branch of theology and must never be allowed to lose its theological dimension.

PART THREE

Some Possibilities for Christology

Introduction

The final part of this book is concerned with the effect that christological belief has on our understanding of God. The first chapter is introductory: it is concerned with the relationship between christology and theology, and seeks to justify the view taken throughout the book that christology has a theological function. The second chapter contains the substance of the theological implications of christology and illustrates areas which are affected when we view christology and theology in this way. The final chapter returns to the question of how such christological thinking is to be expressed and argues for the continued use of the model of revelation.

Christology and Theology

The relation between two types of christology

We have been considering two basic types of christology, those which work from below and those which work from above. It is possible to view these in stark contrast or to see them as complementary.

When viewed in contrast, one type is fundamentally a theology of Jesus of Nazareth. It is concerned with the message and style of life of the man Jesus. We have seen difficulties in this approach. It emphasizes the features of a culturally conditioned life to the exclusion of what he indicates about the character of God.[1] It fails to present a saving christology, for it is not able to sustain the requirements of a doctrine of atonement, simply because it lacks a theocentric concern.[2]

The other type, an approach from above, also presents difficulties, the chief of which is seen in its attempts to make sense of the statement that 'God became man'. For the centre of attention is directed to seeking an explanation of *how* God could become man. This is to confine christology to too narrow a question and to direct it away from the real ontological question 'who is Jesus Christ?'

Some contemporary christology has sought to mingle these two approaches, and there is much merit in a recognition of the complementary nature of these approaches.[3] Isolated they are inadequate; together they can correct each other. The New Testament supports such mutuality, for, broadly speaking, earliest christological thinking moved from a consideration of the humanity of Jesus to a recognition of the place of God in his life, without moving away from a firm historical basis.

In this book, I am seeking a christological approach which, on the one hand, is founded on the historical figure, Jesus of Nazareth, and, on the other hand, sees itself as a servant of theology, designed to further our understanding of the character of God. For christology is designed to stand between a historical study of Jesus of Nazareth and a search for a deeper understanding of God; it begins with Jesus and ends with God.[4]

Christology's theological task

The dispute between jesuology and christology which runs throughout the history of the church and has been acute in recent theology prevents the real task of christology. For in the struggle to hold the balance between the two approaches, the Christian theologian has failed to grasp the vision of God implied in his own christological confession. Neither jesuology nor christology has been equal to this task; jesuology, because it does not recognize the peculiar presence of God in Jesus; christology, because it has seen its description of Jesus Christ as an end in itself. Only a theologically orientated christology, based on the historical figure, can fulfil this task. For the hope of the Christian is not to understand how God and man are related in the person of Jesus Christ; it is to know God, as he has presented himself in Jesus Christ. Therefore a theological christology does not begin by assuming a general concept of God which it imposes on christology. It seeks to allow its concept of God to be challenged, corrected and if necessary rejected by the God who is present in Jesus Christ. Only in this way can a fully Christian understanding of God be derived from the Christian revelation.[5]

This is not to deny that christology has another role to play, namely, that of presenting an influential indication of the nature of man.[6] It could indeed be argued that the prior need today is for man to understand his own humanity. But this cannot be the first objective. An understanding of God is necessary for our understanding of man.[7] Theology is not abstract; it is existential and seeks to answer man's deepest questions. Man's search for God is part of his search for the meaning of human existence, and is the key to that search. The two tasks are interdependent, but the theological role is prior, and this essay is concerned almost exclusively with the theological implications of christology.

The revision of the concept of God

An encounter with Jesus compelled people to examine their presuppositions about God,[8] if only because Jesus spoke more directly about God than was customary. The most important issue concerning Jesus is not to sort out which of the New Testament titles best fits what he or the early Christians thought him to be. The central issue concerns his relationship to God. Did Jesus indicate – by his teaching, activity, prayer – that he had an understanding of, and a relationship with, and a teaching about God which was sufficiently significant to affect our whole understanding of God?[9] This is a key question, and with respect to the historical Jesus it is *the* question. Other christological issues are subsidiary to this. They may be part of the process of building up an answer to this central question, but a preoccupation with them has only served to obscure the theological issue. This has not always been the case: Paul was less concerned with finding the best title and more concerned with expressing his growing conviction that to understand Jesus was to understand God himself.[10]

Christology leads, therefore, to a revision of our concept of God. For christology seeks to present an influential account of God. It will be influential, however, only if it is allowed not so much to be influenced by but rather itself to help to determine our understanding of God. Usually it is theology which determines christology. But then the Christian revelation becomes subject to, and imprisoned by, the inherited doctrine of God. This is largely what happened in post-Nicene controversies over the person of Christ: the mode of the incarnation was the centre of interest and attempts to define the incarnate person largely lost the wider perspective of God's plan for mankind.[11] When christology is at its best it is about God, not about the mode of the incarnation or the make-up of the person of Christ.[12]

My criticism that the Christian concept of God has not been sufficiently influenced by christology is not a rejection of the influence of Greek thought on the development of Christianity and does not support a view that Greek philosophy took over Christianity at an early stage, preventing its development along more proper Hebraic lines. For it is now recognized that pre-Christian Judaism was itself a vehicle for Greek thought and that there was a considerable mingling of Hebraic and Hellenistic conceptions of God before the birth of Christianity.[13] In the continuing interaction between the inherited Greek concept of God and biblical faith, the early fathers were principally concerned to retain biblical monotheism.[14] They therefore embraced Platonic thought, precisely because this provided a means of expressing the absoluteness of God. But the adoption of this Platonic view brought problems, because it involved the concept of God as separate from the world and as an unchanging object.[15] The problem for Christian theology was to integrate the data of the Christian revelation with the notion of God in such Platonic thought. It did this in terms of Christ's pre-existence and his creative role. This did not, however, leave much room for Jesus' understanding of God to influence the church's understanding of what God was like. The development of the divinity of Christ and, later, the doctrine of the trinity remained the church's principal concern, rather than what the Christian God was like in himself.

The relation between christology and theology

The general unwillingness to allow christology to influence theology suggests a need for further clarification of their relationship. The history of Christian theology can be expressed as a story of the effects on the church of the tension between God and Christ, theocentricity and christocentricity. It is well argued that since the seventeenth century stress has increasingly been placed on the figure of Christ. Now it is necessary for the balance to be redressed and for a rediscovery of the sense of God.[16] Early Christian experience can properly be described as being in the first place theocentric in the sense that Christians had a direct relationship with God.[17] The New Testament documents make clear that early Christian experience was also christocentric: believers spoke of themselves as being 'in Christ'; their experience was of the resurrection of Christ. But through this christocentric experience Christians were able to enter into a more direct relationship with the God in whom they already believed.[18] Christians today choose to speak of their experience in a variety of ways – principally, as experience of Christ, the Spirit or God. It is important that those who use the language of Christ or the Spirit to articulate their personal experience do so in such a way that their experience is clearly seen to be experience of God himself. For the most important need today in response to the vague deism of society is to help those who struggle with the mystery of God to discover a *Christian* view of God. To enable this, we must be prepared to give up our inherited concept of God so that a more Christian understanding may prevail.[19]

This replacement of the pre-Christian concept of God (named by some as the god of antiquity) by a concept of God which follows through the implications of christology is a reversal of what normally has happened. In antiquity there is a general understanding of God as intransitory, immortal, unchangeable and impassible.[20] In its desire to preserve the holiness of God it overemphasizes the transcendence and separateness of God. This has meant that the doctrine of the two natures began with the fundamental distinction between the being of God and the nature of man. Our conventions in speaking about God are still to a large extent determined by these historical roots which lie in Hellenistic Judaism rather than in the specifically Christian revelation.[21] Death of God christology tried to break away from this inherited picture of God's transcendence. But it did not realize that an acceptance rather than a denial of the divinity of Christ was the way to achieve the liberation required, a liberation not from belief in God but from the transcendence of God as traditionally conceived. Process theology attempts this liberation too, a liberation from God as the unchanging and passionless absolute. But it seeks to replace the God of antiquity with the God of process philosophy, rather than the God who is seen in Jesus Christ.

The opposite to kenosis

We can further illustrate the nature of what I have called theological christology by recognizing that it is the opposite to modern kenotic christology. The concept of kenosis has been understood in different ways.[22] In patristic theology it did not influence christological theories, and later, when it was connected with the coming of the Logos, it did not refer to the setting aside of divine nature and its attributes but to the assumption of human nature. Even in the seventeenth and eighteenth centuries, Lutheran theologians did not think of Christ's self-denying as a relinquishing of divinity in the incarnation. They used the concept to describe the ways in which the unity with the divine nature was effected. It was not until the nineteenth century, with its self-conscious literalizing of the incarnation, that kenosis came to be understood as the self-emptying of the Logos at the incarnation in the sense of a physical self-limitation of his divinity.

There are fundamental difficulties in this modern kenotic theory. First, in supposing that there are special qualities, attributes or characteristics of God which are not seen in Jesus Christ, kenoticism reflects a traditional, inherited view of God. Second, working within this framework, kenotic theories seek to suggest how God became man. But, as we have seen, this is to literalize the mythological character of the doctrine of the incarnation. Such a literalization does indeed demand either kenoticism or an assertion of two consciousnesses in Jesus Christ. The latter destroys his humanity and divides his person, and the former leads us away from the fundamental Christian insight that Jesus shows us the character of God. Third, kenosis fails in its objective of providing a way out of the difficulties caused by an acceptance, on the one hand, of the traditional dogma that God became man and, on the other hand, of the full humanity of the historical figure. For kenosis is able to allow the humanity of Jesus only to the degree that it denies his divinity. Yet the more complete the self-emptying, the less meaning can be given to the incarnation.[23]

Despite these objections, there is a noticeable reluctance to abandon kenoticism altogether. What might be called a lingering kenoticism remains.[24] There is a reluctance to allow christology to penetrate theological understanding, despite a recognition of the principle that God himself becomes visible in Christ.[25]

The combination of the continuing attractiveness of kenosis and the overwhelming objections to its approach has produced what can only be termed a theory of non-kenotic kenosis. Vanstone acknowledges the strong objections but seeks to overcome them by suggesting that the God who is revealed 'is the very God who "emptied himself" ', by which he means that God's whole and total activity is the activity of self-emptying or kenosis.[26] In this way, he suggests, the kenosis of the redeemer, that is, his surrender of that which he might have held, will be the perfect manifestation of the kenosis of God: the emptiness of Christ, in his poverty and humility, points to the emptiness of God. In this understanding of the relationship between Christ and God, it is clear that the alleged kenosis in Christ does not prevent the full disclosure of God but, on the contrary, expresses the substance of that disclosure. This moving account of God's love experienced in Christ is not therefore a variant of modern kenotic christology. The phrase 'kenosis of God' indicates that what is being described is the very nature of God, not the process by which he became man. For Vanstone believes Christianity should not hesitate in attributing to God that authenticity of love it sees in Christ. As such, his account reflects the christological approach to theology I am advocating here.

– 8 –

Some Implications of a Christological Theology

Introduction

This book is written to promote a more theological understanding of the task of christology, in short, to suggest that all Christian theology is basically christological theology. I have previously spoken of 'theological christology', by which I mean that christology has primarily a theological concern. I now speak of 'christological theology', for I am seeking an understanding of God which is christologically determined. To illustrate, I select three examples of the approach of christological theology, namely, the question of God's omnipotence, together with the problem of evil; soteriology, the study of salvation, together with the question of the suffering of God; and the related areas of worship, prayer and the spiritual life.

The concept of God's omnipotence and the problem of evil

The concept of God used in classical philosophical theism has led to acute difficulties in Christian theology because it is unable to combine the notion of supreme dominion demanded by its concept of God with the infinite love of God illustrated in the life, death and resurrection of Jesus Christ.[1] At the centre of this difficulty is the concept of omnipotence. For in the classical understanding of God, omnipotence has meant God's absolute ability to do everything. This understanding was taken over by expounders of the Christian faith, though it is a pre-Christian notion.

One way of exposing the problem is to ask why the loving God apparently chooses not to do everything he can to express his love.[2] Could not God put right the evils of the world? If he has the power to do all things, why does he not exercise this power in order to make life more bearable? What sort of a God is it who, having the ability, decides to do so little about so many things that are wrong with humanity and creation? These are some of the painful questions inevitably directed towards a God who is understood to be omnipotent.

The stark picture of God's omnipotence in classical theism is inadequate.[3] It can evoke the response of fear and perhaps even some sort of worship, but not that of love. Ironically, it paints a picture of a God who is incomplete, precisely because such an omnipotent God is not able to experience that powerlessness which is the common experience of man. Such understanding of God's omnipotence is therefore inadequate for the purpose of Christian theology, for it involves a denial of the revelation of God given in Jesus Christ.

Christological theology suggests another approach by offering a different understanding of omnipotence. For christological theology does not accept the inherited concept of God's omnipotence. It understands the nature of omnipotence to be determined by the nature of Christ's power. For the incarnation challenges everything people had previously believed about God, including the nature of his omnipotence. The life and death of Jesus Christ illustrate the true nature of power and so indicate the nature of God's power. God's omnipotence therefore cannot be understood apart from the powerlessness experienced by Jesus, particularly as it is seen in the crucifixion.

It is right to draw conclusions from this approach to God's power that affect both the way we think about *man* and the way we think about *God*. On the one hand, the life of Jesus is the supreme ideal for man, even though by human standards it ended in failure and defeat. This leads to the suggestion that in today's world God is to be found most clearly in those human lives which experience oppression, injustice and defeat.[4] On the other hand, theological conclusions also follow. The real sovereignty of God is that of one who has known the humiliation of defeat and relies on the powerlessness of love. This is quite different, however, from the concealment or laying aside of divine power of a kenotic approach, which resists the conclusion that this is what God is really like in himself. The power of the suffering and death of Jesus that arises out of his submissive character indicates the character of God, the nature of his power, and the way in which his power is exercised. For the God who is seen in Jesus Christ chose the way of weakness rather than coercion, because this is his character. In the incarnation, he took the risk of failure and, by the world's standards, did fail.[5] This is why the Christian understanding of God is such a disappointment to those whose prior understanding of God expects a different and more powerful God.

In this context, it is important that the resurrection is not seen as a triumphal reversing of the defeat of the crucifixion, but rather that, together, the cross and the resurrection are seen as both defeat and victory. They are a defeat of the sort of power by which the world judges victory and they are a victory for that power of love which the world judges to be powerlessness.

I am not suggesting that the term 'omnipotence' should be abandoned, but that an understanding of God's power should be determined by the exercise of that power in Jesus Christ. This gives a different meaning to omnipotence. It comes to mean the exercise of such power to the uttermost and the claim that nothing can diminish his love, which leads to the conclusion that the omnipotence of a personal God is seen in his showing mercy and pity and in his creative limitation.[6] It is important, however, to recognize that I am not talking about just the way in which God exercises his power, about the manner of his omnipotence. I am speaking of the very nature of God's power, not just as present in the life of Jesus of Nazareth, but as present in the being of God. This is not to reduce God's omnipotence to an ethical quality. It is to invite the development of an ontology of love in which our understanding of God's powerfulness will be radically different from that inherited by most Christian theology from classical theism.

The problem of evil is related to our consideration of the power of God because God's powerfulness is questioned in the light of man's suffering and the presence of evil in the world. The problem of evil is traditionally expressed in terms of three basic statements: God is good; God is all-powerful; there is evil in the world. The question is properly asked: can the presence of evil in the world be reconciled with the existence of a God who is unlimited both in goodness and power? The phrasing of this question acknowledges that the problem of evil is not a threat to every concept of God. It arises only when religion insists on God as being at once perfectly good and unlimitedly powerful. Traditionally, Christianity has been understood and has understood itself in this way.

We can take as an example of a serious Christian response to the problem of evil the defence of the justice and righteousness of God presented by Hick.[7] Hick does not attempt to deny the reality of evil (a theoretical solution to the problem as presented), but accepts the fact of evil in the world as one of the given factors. Rather does he seek to defend God against the attack that the fact of evil seems to make upon him. His theodicy is expressed in eschatological terms: God is defended in terms of the infinite future good. He argues that in the end we shall come to see that it was for the best that the world is as it is, and that the future will undoubtedly bring the triumph of good over evil. Given the traditional understanding of the problem, such an approach offers a positive way of coming to terms with some of the evil in the world. Evil is recognized; the goodness of God is defended; his omnipotence, as traditionally conceived, goes unchallenged.

If, however, the omnipotence of God is understood along the lines suggested by a christological approach to theology, the nature of the problem changes. It is not now the justice and goodness of God which need to be defended. Rather has the concept of God as one who is not, as traditionally understood, omnipotent to be defended against the suspicion that this is a contradiction in terms. Is it not an attempt to limit his power, to limit God, and so to deny him? A christological understanding of God's omnipotence does not seek to limit the power of God. It offers an understanding of the nature of his power in terms which enable us to account for the continued existence of undefeated evil (though this, it must be said, is not its motive). Evil continues to reign because God is not yet able to overcome it. His power is a power of love, and only in time will love prevail. In the meantime, the confrontation between good and evil is real, and the contribution made by individuals and communities which support either evil or love will really count. This framework retains Hick's eschatological note, but does not require a defence of God's justice.

An illustration of what this means is found in Vanstone's theology of love, where God's activity in creation is seen as precarious, that is, a work of love whose shape cannot be predetermined nor its triumph foreknown. The existence of evil is seen as the consequence of this precariousness in the context of the vulnerability of God's love. Vanstone's thinking is based partly on a reflection on his own experience of creation and love and partly on his refusal to allow the theological legacy he inherited to inhibit the implications of the description of God as love. As such it is an example of christological theology.[8]

Soteriology and the suffering of God

From an early stage soteriology has worked from the dictum that the whole man would not have been saved unless God had taken upon himself the whole man.[9] This working principle reflects the general approach of the New Testament documents and the early Fathers that there is a natural relation between incarnation and atonement. In its outworking, it led to a concentration on the human soul of Jesus and to the defeat of those christologies which sought to deny his human soul. Such a denial did seem possible within the framework of a Logos-sarx christology but was not possible in a Logos-anthropos christology, for, unlike sarx, anthropos includes the human soul. It was therefore partly a different christological framework and partly direct soteriological considerations which led to the firm conclusion of the full humanity of Jesus. This was the central issue on the road to Chalcedon. There, however, reflection ceased. Soteriology and christology had interacted, but little conclusion had been drawn for theology. The concentration had been on the person of Christ as the one through whom salvation came and little attention had been given to the question of God himself as Saviour, or what concept of God such an approach might indicate.

Christological theology has implications that must be worked out in the area of soteriology. We can take the thought of Aulén as a more recent example of the possibility and difficulty of doing this. When Aulén reviews the implications of his dramatic christology for the image of God, he acknowledges that his aim is to explore three caricatures: the God of fatalism (where evil comes from God), the God of moralism (where there is no spontaneity in God's love) and a shallow view of God's love (where love is considered self-evident and there is no conception of love's hard work). Throughout this study, Aulén is therefore concerned with the theological implications of theories of the atonement and reflects the need for our concept of God to match our appreciation of the person and work of Jesus Christ.[10] But Aulén chooses the concept of paradox to express this, suggesting that 'the God, the all-ruler, the Infinite, yet accepts the lowliness of the Incarnation'. This use of paradox suggests that Aulén has not allowed his understanding of the lowliness of Jesus Christ to qualify his preconception of God as the all-ruler, the infinite. The picture of God that emerges is not derived from his appreciation of the incarnate one. Instead resort is made to paradox to account for the difference between the inherited picture of God and the picture of God drawn from the person and work of Jesus Christ.

But the attempt to recover the theological dimension of the atonement is to be welcomed. For, while it is possible to identify the specifically Christian element in our faith as the belief that it is through what Christ has done that forgiveness is available, it is the more important to assert that this belief is justified only if we think of what Christ has done as having been done by God himself.[11] An acknowledgment of the theological nature of the atonement does not lead to a particular theory, but to reflection on the nature and character of God who is himself the agent of atonement. This dimension is often overlooked, and it is probably true to say that most doctrines of the atonement have implied that the Son is more compassionate than the Father.[12]

73

One reason why there has been a reluctance to draw theological conclusions from an understanding of the saving work of Christ is because it raises the question of the suffering of God. This question is raised very directly by the Abelardian treatment of the sacrifice of Christ. Waddell's story of the encounter of Abelard and Thibault with the trapped rabbit tells how Abelard came to recognize that 'God is in it too'. This reference is not just to the suffering of Christ at Calvary but to the very character of God. Imaginatively, this thought has been likened to the story of the prodigal son, in which the father's act of welcome is seen both as a single and particular action and as one which is the focal point of the long-formed character of the Father and an expression of his normal behaviour.[13] These two illustrations (Abelard's encounter and the prodigal son) both suggest by analogy that the suffering of Jesus Christ indicates the suffering of God himself. For the only way a person can show love is to express that love himself; it cannot be done by proxy.

Yet almost all theologies have denied that God can suffer. Behind such theology lies the philosophy of the Greeks, where God is the unmoved mover, the passionless spectator.[14] Despite its affirmation of the divinity of Jesus Christ, Christian theology has denied that it is God who suffered. This, as we have seen, is because the Platonic concept of God was of one separate from the suffering world and himself an unchanging object. Such a God was unable to suffer. But if God himself did not suffer, the claim that God's own love is expressed in Jesus is emptied of meaning: the suffering of another being is not the suffering of God. We must not attempt to use the doctrine of the Trinity as an evasion of this truth. If we claim that the death of Christ is redemptive it is because we acknowledge that we are speaking of the passion of God, for only God has this redemptive power.

What is more important than any of the theories of the atonement, each of which stresses one aspect of an experienced salvation, is that our understanding of atonement is not at variance with our understanding of the nature of God. Let us take sacrifice as an example: once it was realized that it was unworthy of God's self-sufficiency to think he was dependent on sacrifice, this implied understanding of sacrifice was recognized to be unacceptable.[15] Pre-conceived soteriological theory must not be allowed to determine our understanding of God, but our understanding of salvation and how it works, so to speak, must be compatible with our understanding of God, christologically derived. There is continual interaction at this point: the suffering of Christ leads to a deeper understanding of God, and an understanding of the suffering as God's gives further meaning to the suffering of Christ. But in the end it is our christologically derived theology which determines our understanding of the work of Christ. This is not to assert the priority of Christ's person over his work. It is to assert the absolute priority of theology.

Only if *God* is seen to be the Saviour can we speak of salvation in any absolute sense, for the idea that Christ is absolute saviour is dependent on the concept of God's self-communication in him.[16] For only if the event of salvation is God's doing can it have universal meaning. The development seen in the New Testament documents from the description of God as saviour to the acknowledgment of Christ as saviour complements the development of christology in which Christ is recognized as God. Only because of such christological development is it possible to call Christ the saviour, for to do so without such development would be without meaning in a monotheistic faith. Today this theological understanding of salvation provides a context in which the universal claim of salvation in Christ can be discussed with other religions, and in which universalism, in the sense that all will be saved, becomes a possibility.

Traditionally, christology has been preoccupied with presenting the person of Christ in such a way that he can have been an adequate saviour, that is, as fully man and fully God. Whilst this is a proper concern, there lies behind it a more fundamental belief that God is the only and adequate saviour. The narrower christological consideration must never become isolated from the theological, nor allowed to detract from its centrality. Christ is saviour because God is Saviour, and Christ's manner as saviour points to God's character as saviour. The effect of this theological approach is to reassert the sovereignty of God: he is the saviour of the world.

Worship, prayer and the spiritual life

Doctrinal and theological conclusions affect our worship. Any suggestion that certain language about Christ may be appropriate for theological reflection but need not affect our worship is to be rejected.[17] This is not to suggest that language used in theological reflection is necessarily appropriate for worship, but that there is a need for consistency between theology and worship, for both are seeking to discover and express the truth of God. Their positive correspondence works in two directions: not only does doctrine affect worship, but worship may affect the development of doctrine, as in the Arian controversies. Here there was a steady pressure at work on theology from the fact that Christ was worshipped as God.[18] We must therefore include a consideration of worship in this essay, for worship and theology interact on each other.

One clear implication of christological theology is the rejection of the concept of mediator in worship. For if mediator christology is theologically inadequate, it cannot be proper liturgically. It may be a true historical judgment that from the earliest days there was an understanding of Christ's mediatorial role and that the liturgical result of the Arian controversy was that stress was placed on what separates us from God's infinite majesty, a factor which kept alive the mediatorial role of Christ.[19] For it is certainly true that if God is removed out of man's reach to an ineffable majesty, a mediator or series of mediators is required to effect a relationship. This is what happened in post-exilic Judaism, as a result of which the priestly caste became so powerful. In some ways it was the mediator concept which encouraged the development of such a system in Christianity, for the removedness of God from his world and his people was emphasized through the use of language which described Christ as mediator. But it was the retention of a former, pre-Christian concept of God, namely the God of infinite majesty, which led to the creation of a mediatorial need and the development of a mediatorial system. Abandon that concept of God, as christological theology does, and the need to see Christ as mediator has disappeared.

Despite the superficial attractiveness of understanding Christ as mediating human worship to God and divine blessings to human life, the concept is to be rejected. For all too easily the Son, as mediator, becomes, as with Arius, merely a cosmological intermediary, the instrument of God's creative action rather than the revealer of God's nature. It is true, of course, that many who commend the mediator concept do so in the context of full trinitarian theology, and in no way wish to be associated with neo-Arianism. But it is not so clear that mediator theology can adequately guard against this. Trinitarian theology should never be used to avoid the implication of a christologically controlled approach to the nature of God. If God is as he shows himself to be in Jesus Christ, he is himself accessible and there is no need for any mediator.[20]

It is clear that it is an inadequate concept of God which fosters the need for a mediator. For mediators appear necessary in the history of religion only when God becomes increasingly abstract and remote. In this situation the mediator figure enables man to express his desire to experience God in a more concrete way than an abstract understanding of God allows. The function of this mediator is to bridge the gulf between the infinite and the finite and to bring reunion between infinite God and finite man.[21] Ironically, the development of a mediator idea only serves to remove God further from his creation, for apart from that presupposition the mediator has no function.

The basic issue is that of God's presence in Jesus Christ. Mediator christology has no concept of the immediate presence of God himself in Jesus. Christological theology on the other hand affirms that in Jesus Christ God himself was present. With such a God a mediator is superfluous, both theologically and liturgically.[22]

A further illustration of the effect of christological theology on our worship is seen through the response made to the question 'should Christ be worshipped?' The worship of Christ is a common experience in the life of the church. But there can be no justification for it in mediator christology, for such a Christ is only the alleged means through whom God is approached, not God himself. Worship of such a Christ would be idolatry, for God alone is worthy of worship. Worship of Christ therefore is acceptable only when it is a deliberate expression of the worship of God, that is, of the God who has shown himself in Christ and who is present in Christ. Only a strictly theological context can rescue the worship of Christ from a cult of humanity: he who sees me sees the Father. Christological theology does not therefore reject the practice of worshipping Christ; on the contrary, it provides the framework within which it is acceptable. In terms of the real presence of Christ at the Lord's supper, this means that an assertion of real presence is an assertion of the real presence of God, and it is God's real presence which creates the worship and the adoration.

Similarly, our understanding of prayer is determined by our concept of God. For example, a recognition that God's omnipotence is a weakness of power affects our understanding of intercession. For if God is not all-powerful in the way the world understands power, he should not be addressed in prayer as though he is able to order the affairs of the world as a favour to those who ask him.[23] Such a practice in any case suggest that there is a relationship of privilege between God and his supporters. Jesus taught that God deals with people impartially and cannot be manipulated for man's own ends. When intercession has this implication, it has become fundamentally unchristian; that is, it does not reflect the specifically Christian understanding of God and is not addressed to the God whose presence is seen in Jesus Christ. Intercessory prayer can be a much richer experience, a sharing with God in weakness and a seeking of the best in the particular circumstances together with God. A shift of emphasis from the power of God to those qualities revealed in Jesus Christ would also lead us to understand the heart of prayer in terms other than intercession.

A further illustration concerns the use of the phrase 'through Jesus Christ'. This phrase lends itself too easily to a mediatorial interpretation. Its constant use at the conclusion of prayers gives the appearance that the prayer is offered through the mediation of Christ, as though it would be improper, or even impossible, to approach God directly. But if we allow our understanding of God to be determined by what Jesus Christ indicates, there is no question of God being an unapproachable, inaccessible being. He is 'dear father', to whom men and women can speak quite directly. The phrase 'through Jesus Christ' can more properly be taken to suggest that the prayer is being made to the God who is known to us through Jesus Christ, that is, through the life, death and resurrection of Jesus Christ. But ambiguity would be avoided if an alternative closing phrase were used, such as 'in the name of Jesus Christ' or 'for the sake of Jesus Christ', phrases which do not lend themselves quite so readily to a mediatorial interpretation. For if we pray in mediatorial language we shall come to think of God in those terms too.

Finally, we can consider an implication of christological theology in the area of the spiritual life, namely, the question of imitation. There are dangers in seeing the life of the Christian as an imitation of Jesus Christ. Such an approach can very easily become an imitation of his alleged human characteristics and thus an expression of jesuology. Or it can become fastened to some alleged teaching of Jesus, such as pacifism or revolution. If, however, we have rejected jesuology, we must reject such imitation of Jesus as the basis of Christian spirituality. Moreover, this same argument is applicable to christology as well: if christology as an end in itself is rejected, imitation of Christ as an end in itself is unacceptable too. Use of Philippians 2, for example, as a call to the imitation of the pattern of Christ's salvation-life, is inadequate unless the passage is used to point to the means God chose to express himself, a means which illustrates his essential character. Even this important dying and rising motif loses its value if it is unrelated to the imitation of God. For in the New Testament, imitation is not presented as an isolated devotion to Jesus Christ as the model hero for the believer, but is to be found in a fuller trinitarian setting.[24] The Christian theme of imitation is at its best, therefore, when it is expressed as the imitation of God, as seen in Jesus Christ. It then avoids both jesuology, the imitation of a merely human characteristic, and christology, a christocentricism which does not belong to the higher levels of faith, and also meets the challenge of other religions in which men and women also seek to imitate God.

— 9 —

The Model of Revelation

The search for a model

We must now return from a consideration of some of the possible implications of a theological understanding of christology to the narrower subject of christology itself. Christology is concerned both with the relationship between Christ and God and with the way this relationship is to be expressed. We shall want to approach this question in the light of a theological understanding of the role of christology and ask what model or models should be used in such a christological expression. We are committed to a way of expressing the relationship between God and Christ which neither minimizes Christ, and so separates a study of Jesus from christology, nor absolutizes Christ, and so separates christology from theology. Our basic pattern is a christology which is founded on the historical figure, but which points forward to a deeper understanding of God.

The search for a model brings much of this study into focus. For in speaking in Part One about various trends in contemporary christology I was considering a variety of models that have been used to express understanding of the person of Christ. And in Part Two I reflected on models that are used in the New Testament documents, particularly those of 'event' and 'person' christologies. The use of a model is necessary because of the nature of theological language. Talk about God cannot be either as direct or as precise as talk about a personal friend who is known also to those whom we are addressing. The model is not designed to stand in between us and God, but rather to be a more or less adequate way of expressing intelligently and coherently our experience and thought about him. The search for a christological model arises out of the conviction of the centrality of Jesus Christ for our knowledge of God. Apart from this conviction there would be no compelling need for christology at all and no need therefore for christological models.

But what sort of models are we looking for? Christology is concerned

with two sorts of models. It looks for models to describe the person of
Christ and it is concerned with affirming that Christ is a model of God.
This distinction corresponds to the distinction between picturing models,
which endeavour to be replicas of reality, and disclosure models, which
are the media through which reality discloses itself.[1] A theological understanding of christology will be primarily concerned with the latter, for
I have argued that it has been christology's limited concern with the
former which has prevented it from influencing our concept of God and
so fulfilling its central theological task. This strongly suggests that the
basic christological model, a disclosure model, is that of revelation. For,
theologically understood, the christological material needs the revelation
model to do justice to its role.

The basic model of revelation is itself, however, expressed in a variety
of ways, thus fulfilling the need for a plurality of models.[2] Logos, Son of
God and Spirit are all instances of revelational models. They exercise a
function complementary to each other. They could all be described as
models of the incarnation,[3] but are better seen simply as examples of
possible revelational models. They cluster around the central concept of
revelation, illustrating its basic claim that God was revealed in Jesus
Christ, but on their own are insufficient to express the fullness of this
claim. Revelation is to be preferred as a more basic model than incarnation
in the sense that it was the concept of revelation which prepared the
ground for the doctrine of the incarnation.

The idea of revelation

The idea of revelation has been used in different ways in Christian thinking. It has been used to refer to the words in the Bible, the events in
scripture, a body of doctrine or an encounter with God. What exactly do
I mean when I speak of the primacy of the model of revelation? Although
in its widest sense the word may be used to signify the conveying of
information, in the biblical documents it is not used of trivial information
but reserved for the revelation of a mystery, namely the mystery of God's
own purpose.[4] In the Old Testament, this is the unveiling of God's
essential hiddenness; in the New Testament it is the self-disclosure of
God. It is this meaning of divine self-disclosure that enables its use in a
theological christology. For Jesus did not reveal information about God,
not even about his love and forgiveness; he is rather the self-revelation or
self-disclosure of God.[5]

This is how the New Testament documents understand the revelation
of God in Jesus Christ, despite the relatively few explicit expressions of

the concept of revelation to be found there outside the Fourth Gospel. Even in John, not much use is made of the technical terminology of revelation, but the theme is central to the Gospel. It finds its clearest expression in the Logos of the prologue and is expounded in terms of sonship in the body of the Gospel.[6] These two models of Logos and Sonship, two of the most fundamental models of revelation, are used in a complementary manner in John: the one is used to expound the meaning of the other. The result is John's affirmation: he who sees Jesus sees the Father.

In the New Testament, as most clearly expressed in John's Gospel, revelation is given through a person, Jesus Christ, and through events in his life. The person and the events are both apprehended by faith as the mighty acts of God.[7] A biblical understanding of revelation, therefore, requires a recognition both of the historical life of Jesus, such as I have argued is the necessary basis for any constructive christology, and of the part played by faith. For the conviction that God has revealed himself in Jesus Christ rests on a certain response to his person and a certain understanding of the events of his life, namely, seeing them with the eye of faith. Then the revelation in Jesus Christ is the clue to the understanding of everything else.[8] But the revelation has to be received; it has the power of revealing only to those who respond, as is well illustrated in the ministry of Jesus.

Objections to revelation

Marked scepticism has been expressed about the use of the term 'revelation'.[9] It is alleged that it is not a proper term to use either of the biblical material or of the Christian faith as usually expounded, for the idea of revelation is neither biblical nor meaningful. At the very least, it is suggested, the biblical material on the one hand and the philosophical meaning on the other suggests that the term is in need of such qualification that it would be less confusing to use another word. As there is much that we do not know about God, the argument continues, revelation is simply too grand a word. Moreover, as room must in any case be found for 'natural-revelation', the concept of revelation is not necessary as a safeguard of the real distinctiveness of the Christian faith. For, if Jesus is seen as the supreme example of God's working in all men, the term has been evacuated of all meaning.

It is not my task to defend an inappropriate use of the term revelation, but rather to show that the concept of revelation is most appropriate for christological theology. For it is true that much Christian theology that has made use of the concept of revelation has not taken sufficiently seriously the implicit claim that God is as he is shown to be in Jesus Christ. But the purpose of this book is precisely to commend the taking of this seriously through the development of a more Christian understanding of God. For it is the theological implication of christology which demands the use of the model of revelation as the most appropriate way of expressing the belief that the concept of God needs revision in the light of Jesus Christ. The basis of this enterprise is the conviction that the eschaton is present in Jesus Christ, through whom God himself is made known. I am speaking, therefore, of a knowledge of God's essential character and nature, not of a narrowly intellectual knowledge of God, a neo-gnosticism.

This is why I wish to assert the priority of the model of revelation over that of salvation. For to suggest that it is more important to know that we are saved than to know God, treats knowledge of God as a form of esoteric gnosticism. Of course, the two models are complementary and must cohere. But use of revelation as the primary model includes rather than excludes the death of Jesus, as part of a treatment of the total person of Christ and the total event of his revelation. Moltmann's treatment of the crucifixion as an indicator of the nature of God, 'the crucified God', shows how it is possible to integrate the model of salvation into that of revelation.[10] The models are complementary, but the idea of revelation is the more basic because full salvation rests on the revelatory presence of God in Jesus Christ.

Use of the model

The model of revelation may appear to suggest a christological approach from above. The two basic approaches, from above and from below, can, however, be quite properly combined in the use of the model of revelation, as the writings of Paul and John suggest. For these New Testament writers regard the human nature of Jesus Christ as the essential medium of the revelation of God. For them, it is not that God is revealed in Christ despite the conditions of his humanity, but that the essence of his divinity is revealed in the human life.[11]

If use of the model of revelation leads to a doctrine of the incarnation, as we have suggested, let us consider the effects of the use of the model on the doctrine of the Trinity. Trinitarian thought expresses the belief that it was God who was revealing himself in Jesus Christ.[12] Incarnation and Trinity therefore belong together, and if set in the context of God's self-revelation, the bond between them will not be dissolved. Moreover, the model of revelation leads christology to move beyond itself to a consideration of the nature of God. This will eventually lead to 'a developed christological doctrine of the Trinity'.[13] In turn, putting the christological revelation in a trinitarian setting broadens the revelatory base and the incarnation becomes the revelation of the threefold God.[14]

This makes it clear that the model of revelation is not to be used as a technique to remove God's incomprehensibility and mystery. The eschatological dimension of the doctrine of the Trinity enables us to see that revelation, though final, must not be absolutized; that revelation, though God's self-communication, is a promise which points away from Jesus Christ to the character of the self-revealing yet mysterious God. The mystery of God is not reduced by his self-communication, for revelation is both a clarification and a deepening of mystery.[15] The life, death and resurrection of Jesus Christ point to the mystery of God's love, God's suffering, God's self-giving. Christological theology does not seek to by-pass man's inability to perceive and express the incomprehensible and the inexpressible, but rather to be aware of the hiddenness of the God who has made himself known in Jesus Christ.[16]

Revelation 'works', however, only when it is received. Without its reception it does not become revelation. For there are two sides to revelation, an objective side and a subjective side. The reception of God's self-communication in Jesus Christ completes the process of revelation. The Christian religion, therefore, has always rightly been concerned with the question of how revelation is received by the individual and within the Christian community. The history of Christianity indicates a wide variety of experience. This book is not the place even to begin to discuss the importance of this complex subject. Its sole aim is to argue that, in the Christian tradition, the reception of God's initiative in Jesus Christ is recognized as the revelation of God himself.

Conclusion

This book began with a description of some trends in recent christology, followed by a consideration of some of the more important problems raised. In Part Three, a suggestion was made about the way in which christology should be seen if it is to fulfil its theological task. This led to the terms 'theological christology', to express the theological function of christology, and 'christological theology', to indicate the product of such an approach, namely, an understanding of God determined from a christological point of view, or, to put it more directly, a Christian view of God. In conclusion we can ask how this approach enables us to respond to the traditional christological problems.

Christological theology provides a context in which it is possible to speak of uniqueness without denying God's revelation elsewhere. For in shifting the emphasis from Christ to God it encourages us to see that it is God who is at the centre of the universe of faiths.[1] The claim therefore of universal uniqueness is a claim made neither about Jesus of Nazareth nor Jesus Christ. It is a claim made about God. But, for the Christian, the God about whom the claim is made is the God who has made himself known in Jesus Christ. This is because the Christian's understanding of God is always christologically derived. Other knowledge of God's revelation is not to be denied, but the definiteness of Jesus Christ as the determinative source of the Christian knowledge of God is to be affirmed.

A theological view of christology does not dissolve the problem of the historical Jesus, nor does the attempt to put God back on the centre of the stage minimize the claims made about Jesus Christ. On the contrary, a theological emphasis only heightens the question of whether the figure of Jesus of Nazareth can support the claim that God is declared in him. For the Christian this is ultimately a judgment of faith, for the decision to live as though God is as he is seen to be in Jesus Christ is an act of faith taken by each person within the community of those who believe. Such

84

faith is supported by what we know of the historical figure, and it is confirmed when it leads to encounter with God and a deeper knowledge of him.

This is the pattern which is witnessed to in the New Testament documents. A theological christology is confirmed by the twofold emphasis of scripture in refusing to deny the historical and in affirming the ultimate significance of the theological. Any attempt to assign a special place to Jesus but to neglect his special relationship with and to God is to distort the New Testament picture, as well as to raise the question why a religion should be so preoccupied with Jesus of Nazareth. The New Testament affirms the theological character of both what Jesus was doing and who he was in himself. Christology can do no less.

This book has been written in response to the needs of those in our contemporary society who cling to a vague, undefined notion of God but do not know who he is. They might expect to find encouragement from the Christian church to turn this vague wondering into a religious quest to know God more. Often they have not found the Christian church helpful. There may be a variety of reasons for this, including distrust of the institutional character of the church, scepticism about whether Christianity really works, and the phenomenon of human suffering. For the church to be able to respond to the needs of those who enquire after God, it is vital that it should have a clear, distinctive, Christian understanding of God to share with people. This book, in calling for a more christological understanding of God, hopes to make some small contribution in that direction.

Bibliography

G. Aulén, *Christus Victor*, SPCK 1970

D. M. Baillie, *God Was in Christ*, Faber 1948

J. A. Baker, *The Foolishness of God*, Darton, Longman and Todd 1970

M. Black, *A Survey of Christological Thought, 1872–1972*, St Andrew Press 1972

D. Bonhoeffer, *Christology*, Collins 1966

J. M. Creed, *The Divinity of Jesus Christ*, Fontana Books 1964

O. Cullmann, *The Christology of the New Testament*, SCM Press 1959

J. D. G. Dunn, *Christology in the Making*, SCM Press 1980

R. H. Fuller, *The Foundations of New Testament Christology*, Fontana Books 1969

M. D. Goulder (ed.), *Incarnation and Myth*, SCM Press 1979

A. Grillmeier, *Christ in Christian Tradition*, Mowbrays 1975

A. T. Hanson, *Grace and Truth*, SPCK 1975

R. P. C. Hanson, *The Attractiveness of God*, SPCK 1973

A. E. Harvey, *Jesus and the Constraints of History*, Duckworth 1982

M. Hengel, *The Son of God*, SCM Press 1976

J. Hick (ed.), *The Myth of God Incarnate*, SCM Press 1977

J. Hick and B. Hebblethwaite (eds.), *Christianity and Other Religions*, Fount Books 1980

J. Hick, *God and the Universe of Faiths*, Macmillan 1973

J. Knox, *The Humanity and Divinity of Christ*, Cambridge University Press 1967

G. W. H. Lampe, *God as Spirit*, Oxford University Press 1966

N. Lash, *Change in Focus*, Sheed and Ward 1973

J. McIntyre, *The Shape of Christology*, SCM Press 1966

W. R. Matthews, *The Problem of Christ in the Twentieth Century*, Oxford University Press 1950

Bibliography

J. Meyendorff, *Christ in Eastern Christian Thought*, St Vladimir's Seminary, New York 1975

J. Milet, *God or Christ?*, SCM Press 1981

J. Moltmann, *The Crucified God*, SCM Press 1974

C. F. D. Moule, *The Origin of Christology*, Cambridge University Press 1977

C. F. D. Moule, 'Is Christ Unique?', in *Fact, Faith and Fantasy*, Fontana Books 1964

A. Nichols, *The Art of God Incarnate*, Darton, Longman and Todd 1980

W. Pannenberg, *Jesus – God and Man*, SCM Press 1968

N. Pittenger, *Christology Reconsidered*, SCM Press 1970

N. Pittenger (ed.), *Christ for us Today*, SCM Press 1968

K. Rahner, *Foundations of Christian Faith*, Darton, Longman and Todd 1978

K. Rahner and W. Thüsing, *A New Christology*, Burns and Oates 1980

J. A. T. Robinson, *The Human Face of God*, SCM Press 1973

J. A. T. Robinson, *Truth is Two-Eyed*, SCM Press 1979

J. M. Robinson, *A New Quest of the Historical Jesus*, SCM Press 1959

E. Schillebeeckx, *Jesus: An Experiment in Christology*, Collins 1979

E. Schillebeeckx, *Christ: The Christian Experience in the Modern World*, SCM Press 1980

F. D. E. Schleiermacher, *The Christian Faith*, T. and T. Clark 1928

P. Schoonenberg, *The Christ*, Sheed and Ward 1971

A. Schweitzer, *The Quest of the Historical Jesus*, A. and C. Black 1964

J. Sobrino, *Christology at the Crossroads*, SCM Press 1978

S. W. Sykes and J. P. Clayton (ed.), *Christ, Faith and History*, Cambridge University Press 1972

L. S. Thornton, *The Incarnate Lord*, Longmans Green 1928

P. Tillich, *Perspectives on Nineteenth and Twentieth Century Protestant Theology*, SCM Press 1967

P. Tillich, *Systematic Theology*, Vol. I, Nisbet 1953

P. Tillich, *Systematic Theology*, Vol. II, Nisbet 1957

P. Tillich, *Systematic Theology*, Vol. III, Nisbet 1964

W. H. Vanstone, *Love's Endeavour, Love's Expense*, Darton, Longman and Todd 1977

G. Wainwright, *Doxology*, Epworth Press 1980

M. F. Wiles, *The Making of Christian Doctrine*, Cambridge University Press 1967

M. F. Wiles, *The Remaking of Christian Doctrine*, SCM Press 1974

M. F. Wiles, *Working Papers in Doctrine*, SCM Press 1976

F. Young, *Sacrifice and the Death of Christ*, SPCK 1975

Notes

Part One

Introduction

1. This is why Creed began his christology with a study of Schleiermacher's thought. See J. M. Creed, *The Divinity of Jesus Christ*, Fontana Books 1964. F. D. E. Schleiermacher (1768–1834), a German theologian, sought to commend the Christian faith independent of its dogmas. He described religion as a feeling of absolute dependence. See *The Christian Faith*, T. and T. Clark 1928, especially paras. 14 and 96, for his criticism of the traditional doctrine.

2. See, especially, J. Hick (ed.), *The Myth of God Incarnate*, SCM Press 1977, and M. Goulder (ed.), *Incarnation and Myth*, SCM Press 1979.

3. G. W. F. Hegel (1770–1831), a German idealist philosopher, developed a logic of becoming rather than mere being.

4. A Ritschl (1822–89), a German theologian, argued that we apprehend religion by faith rather than by reason. He used the phrase 'value-judgment' because he believed that Christ's divinity could not be proved to those who have not first experienced his saving influence: we know Christ, he argued, only through what he has done for us. See *Justification and Reconciliation*, T. and T. Clark 1900, especially pp. 451ff.

5. For a fuller account of the influence of Schleiermacher, Hegel and Ritschl, see Creed, op. cit. Two further, more recent works are also useful in providing a historical setting for our study: W. R. Matthews, *The Problem of Christ in the Twneiteth Century*, Oxford University Press 1950, and L. B. Smedes, *The Incarnation: Trends in Modern Anglican Thought*, J. H. Kok, Kampen 1955.

6. The term 'nature language' has no relation to what is called 'natural theology', that is, the body of knowledge about God which is obtained by human reason alone. Rather does it simply refer to the use of the classical term 'nature' to describe the human and the divine in the person of Jesus Christ. Its use culminated in the Chalcedonian Definition of 'one Christ in two natures'.

Chapter 1

1. D. M. Baillie, *God Was in Christ*, Faber 1948, p. 87.

2. J. Knox, *The Humanity and Divinity of Christ*, Cambridge University Press 1967, esp. pp. 64, 106.

3. J. A. T. Robinson, *The Human Face of God*, SCM Press 1973. See also N. Pittenger, *Christology Reconsidered*, SCM Press 1970.

4. D. M. Baillie, op. cit., p. 19.

5. K. Barth, *The Humanity of God*, Collins 1961, p. 41. Barth argues that he was right to expound the deity of God, but wrong to view it 'in isolation, abstracted and absolutized, and set . . . over against men'.

6. See M. Black, *A Survey of Christological Thought 1872–1972*, St Andrew Press 1972.

7. G. Vermes, *Jesus the Jew*, Collins 1973.

8. M. Machovec, *A Marxist Looks at Jesus*, Darton, Longman and Todd 1976, p. 119. See also V. Gardavsky, *God is Not Yet Dead*, Pelican Books 1973, and R. Garaudy, *The Alternative Future*, Simon and Schuster, New York 1974.

9. So B. Hebblethwaite in his introduction to Machovec's book.

10. See J. Macquarrie, 'The Humanity of Christ', *Theology*, June 1971, p. 249.

11. J. A. Baker, *The Foolishness of God*, Darton, Longman and Todd 1970, p. 163.

12. Ibid., p. 242.

13. W. Pannenberg, *Jesus – God and Man*, SCM Press 1968, p. 189. Compare E. Schillebeeckx, *Jesus: An Experiment in Christology*, Collins 1979, who opens his study with a post-resurrection story, Acts 3, and treats the resurrection as part of the 'impression that Jesus made on his disciples'.

14. So S. W. Sykes, 'The Theology of the Humanity of Christ', S. W. Sykes and J. P. Clayton (eds.), *Christ, Faith and History*, Cambridge University Press 1972, p. 72, who argues thus because he judges that the resultant christology is somewhat independent of the history or life of Jesus.

15. This appears to be the case in R. P. C. Hanson, *The Attractiveness of God*, SPCK 1973, p. 109, who quickly moves from the claim that 'through his humanity his divinity can be perceived' to the conclusion that 'Jesus is the self-communication of God, and therefore is God'. He supports this argument by reference to Pannenberg's theology and Baillie's analogy of divine grace. But the way his argument is presented shows that it is not easy to move convincingly from a consideration of the humanity of Jesus to the claim that he is the self-communication of God.

16. A. T. Hanson, *Grace and Truth*, SPCK 1975, p. 76, who argues that, as you cannot recognize people 'unless you have seen them before, or heard a description of them, or learned something about them', those who recognize God in Christ must have some previous knowledge of God. Another way of tackling the problem of 'recognition' is suggested in J. Sobrino, *Christology at the Crossroads*, SCM Press 1978, p. 105, who argues that Jesus revealed the way of the Son and Christians came to know this in following the path of his faith. Because Sobrino makes a lesser claim about Jesus (he does not reveal the Father, but only the Son, or the way of the Son), he is left with less of a 'gap' between the claims he is able to make about the human life of Jesus and the christological conclusion he wishes to affirm. Compare L. Boff, *Jesus Christ Liberator*, SPCK 1980.

17. E. L. Mascall, *Theology and the Gospel of Christ*, SPCK 1977, p. 130. See also *Christ, the Christian and the Church*, Longmans 1946. The criticisms of christology from below in the following paragraph are those made by Mascall.

18. D. M. Baillie, op. cit., p. 87.

19. H. M. Relton, *A Study in Christology*, SPCK 1917, who argues that it was

as God that Jesus Christ was perfect man. Compare R. C. Moberley, *Atonement and Personality*, Murray 1901, who argues that Christ was not generically but inclusively man: 'the root and origin of his personality may not be human' (p. 86).

20. See D. B. Evans, *Leontius of Byzantium, An Origenist Christology*, Harvard University Press 1970, though challenged by B. Daley, 'The Origenism of Leontius of Byzantium', *Journal of Theological Studies*, October 1976, pp. 333–69. Leontius' solution (*Contra Nestorianos et Eutychianos*, PG 86, 1276D 5–7; 1277 C14) has received much criticism because it has generally been interpreted as an attempt to restate the Chalcedonian decision along the lines of Cyril's teaching, that is, as a form of anhypostasia. But Evans has argued that Leontius' thought should be interpreted in terms of Origen's thought. He cites texts to indicate that Leontius did not teach that only the human nature is enhypostasized, but that both natures of Christ are enhypostasized. Previous attempts (see note above) to revive the doctrine of enhypostasis have interpreted it on anhypostatic lines. Evans offers a fresh interpretation which fully safe-guards the manhood of Jesus.

21. E. Schillebeeckx, *Jesus*, pp. 653–4.

22. Compare P. Schoonenberg, *The Christ*, Sheed and Ward 1971, to whose thought Schillebeeckx refers.

23. H. P. Owen, 'The New Testament and the Incarnation: A Study in Doctrinal Development', *Religious Studies*, Vol. 8, 1972, p. 222.

24. J. Sobrino, op. cit., p. xvi. Compare Schillebeeckx, who not only states the principle, but also devotes a great deal of his *Jesus* to biblical study, building up a picture of the historical Jesus on which he can base his christology.

25. D. Bonhoeffer, *Christology*, Collins 1966, p. 44.

26. Ebionism denied the divinity of Christ through its claim that Jesus was a normal man born of Joseph and Mary, though predestined Messiah who would return to reign on earth. Compare Paul of Samosata, who used the phrase 'from below' in his exposition of a christology based on the ordinary human nature of Jesus. See A. Grillmeier, *Christ in Christian Tradition*, Mowbrays 1975, p. 165, for a full discussion.

27. J. Meyendorff, *Christ in Eastern Christian Thought*, St Vladimir's Seminary, New York 1975, may judge that the approach from below to the mystery of Christ is the point when the post-Chalcedonian Byzantine thought meets the modern christological concern, but in fact much christology from below fails to achieve that divinization of human nature so central to Byzantine christology.

28. So E. L. Mascall, *Theology and the Gospel of Christ*, SPCK 1977, p. 133, who argues that the problem of uniqueness is acute if Jesus is not accepted as being hypostatically divine.

29. So Lessing, *Lessing's Theological Writings*, ed. H. Chadwick, A. & C. Black 1956, who asks how any particular facts of history can have universal meaning. This basic problem is explored in a wide variety of ways; for example, in psychological terms it becomes a question of the relation of the mind of Jesus to the mind of God. See R. P. C. Hanson, *The Attractiveness of God*, p. 109. But a change of language does not dissolve the problem. Mascall is right to comment on Hick's restatement of Chalcedon (J. Hick, 'Christology at the

Notes

Crossroads', in F. G. Healey (ed.), *Prospect for Theology*, Nisbet 1966) in terms of *agape* that 'there would seem to be metaphysical problems in the assertion that Jesus's *agape* was actually and literally God's *agape* at least as great as ... *ousia*' (*Theology and the Gospel of God*, pp. 122f.).

30. The term is used by J. Hick, op. cit. Compare M. Wiles, 'Christianity without Incarnation', in *The Myth of God Incarnate*, pp. 1–10.

Chapter 2

1. A term used of D. M. Baillie's christology by J. Hick, 'Christology at the Crossroads'. See also M. Wiles, 'In Defence of Arius', in *Working Papers in Doctrine*, SCM Press 1976, pp. 28–37.

2. F. Schleiermacher, op. cit., p. 392.

3. W. Pannenberg, op. cit., p. 284, who believes that it is from the theory of the two natures that all the insoluble problems result.

4. So J. Sobrino, *Christology at the Crossroads*, p. 330.

5. D. Bonhoeffer, *Christology*, pp. 101f.

6. J. McIntyre, *The Shape of Christology*, SCM Press 1966, pp. 102ff. This phrase arises out of McIntyre's consideration of Sartre's preference for 'human condition' to 'human nature'.

7. P. Tillich, *Systematic Theology*, Vol. II, Nisbet 1957, p. 164, and 'A Reinterpretation of the Doctrine of the Incarnation', *Church Quarterly Review* 1948, p. 138.

8. G. C. Stead, *Divine Substance*, Clarendon Press 1977, who argues that the term *physis*, even in Aristotle, could mean 'an immanent formative principle that controls the development of living things' (p. 71). He concludes his detailed examination of the language of substance with the judgment that 'to characterize God as substance is to stake a claim against reductionist theories' (pp. 274f.). Compare C. J. E. Williams, 'A Programme for Christology', *Religious Studies* 3, 1968, p. 517, who recommends that the Aristotelian tool be taken up again.

9. Origen, *Contra Celsum*, ed. H. Chadwick, Cambridge University Press 1953, IV, 18. See A. Grillmeier, *Christ in Christian Tradition*, p. 105, for a full discussion.

10. Stead, op. cit., pp. 274–5.

11. W. Pannenberg, op. cit., p. 35.

12. G. Hendry, *The Gospel of the Incarnation*, SCM Press 1959, p. 25, who comments that it was the Eastern church's preoccupation with the doctrine of the incarnation which led to Chalcedon's concern with the terms of the hypostatic union.

13. D. Cupitt, 'Mr Hebblethwaite on the Incarnation', *Incarnation and Myth*, p. 43, who comments that the classical doctrine has broken down 'because better understanding of the principles of historical judgment, of Jewish thought, and of the literary character of the gospels has fatally weakened the traditional arguments for Jesus' divinity', by which he means his fulfilment of prophecy, his miracles and his sinlessness.

14. J. A. Baker, *The Foolishness of God*, pp. 34–7. Compare J. W. Rogerson, 'Slippery Words, V, Myth', *Expository Times*, October 1978, pp. 10–14, who, in

a similar account, examines four main approaches to what myth has been thought to be.

15. E. Brunner, *The Mediator*, Lutterworth Press 1934, p. 379.

16. A. Grillmeier, op. cit., pp. 64f., commenting on R. Bultmann, *Kerygma and Myth*, SPCK 1953.

17. Compare J. W. Rogerson, op. cit.

18. See P. Tillich, *Perspectives on Nineteenth and Twentieth Century Protestant Theology*, SCM Press 1967, pp. 227ff.

19. So F. Young, 'Incarnation and Atonement: God Suffered and Died', *Incarnation and Myth*, p. 102.

20. So J. Mark, 'Myth and Truth', *Theology*, July 1980, p. 266.

21. So J. W. Rogerson, op. cit.

22. So H. P. Owen, 'The Person of Christ in Recent Theology', *Religious Studies* 13, 1977, p. 498.

23. Wiles' distinction between two stories, the human and the mythological, the man language and the God language, is an illustration of this tendency (M. Wiles, 'Does Christology Rest on a Mistake?') Compare R. A. Norris, 'Towards a Contemporary Interpretation of the Chalcedonian Definition', *Lux in Lumine: Essays to Honour W. Norman Pittenger*, Seabury Press, New York 1966, p. 79, whom J. A. T. Robinson, *The Human Face of God*, quotes with approval. Despite this interest in language, there is no acknowledgment (such as is found in B. Lonergan, 'The Dehellenization of Dogma', *A Second Collection*, Darton, Longman and Todd 1974, p. 23) that the Fathers were using the concept 'substance' metaphorically. Moreover, Wiles' suggestion, 'Christianity Without Incarnation', *The Myth of God Incarnate*, pp. 6f., that to abandon the concept of incarnation would not affect Christian faith much, suggests that the value of the second story, the mythological approach, has quickly been abandoned.

24. W. Pannenberg, *Jesus – God and Man*, pp. 155–6.

25. J. A. Baker, *The Foolishness of God*, p. 308.

26. B. Hebblethwaite, 'The Propriety of the Doctrine of the Incarnation', *Scottish Journal of Theology* 33, June 1980, pp. 216f., who quotes N. Smart, 'Gods, Bliss and Morality', in *Christian Ethics and Contemporary Philosophy*, ed. I. T. Ramsey, SCM Press 1966, p. 25, to the effect that only if heaven and Galilee are both places in the same sense of 'place' would it be a contradiction to say that Christ was in Galilee while God is in heaven, and that Christ is God. See also B. Hebblethwaite, 'Incarnation – the Essence of Christianity?', *Theology*, March 1977, pp. 86f.

27. For a fuller discussion of kenotic christology, see Chapter 7.

28. K. Popper, *The Logic of Scientific Discovery*, Hutchinson 1972.

29. B. Cooper, 'Metaphysics, Christology and Sexism: an Essay in Philosophical Theology', *Religious Studies* 16, 1980, p. 180, who concludes that, because a Whiteheadian view analyses the chief difficulty in traditional christology as lying in its forbidding any way of relating the divine and the human in Jesus except externally, it develops a christology which expresses their internal as well as external relation, with love as the key to the incarnation.

Chapter 3

1. A. N. Whitehead (1861–1947) was associated with the development of modern mathematical logic but later sought a more comprehensive synthesis of knowledge, a philosophy of organism. See *Process and Reality*, Cambridge University Press 1926.

2. D. A. Pailin, 'Incarnation as a Continuing Reality', *Religious Studies* 16, 1980, p. 303.

3. J. B. Cobb and D. R. Griffin, *Process Theology*, Christian Journals 1977, p. 105.

4. See C. Hartshorne, *Man's Vision of God*, Harper, New York 1941, and *The Divine Reality*, Yale University Press 1948.

5. L. S. Thornton, *The Incarnate Lord*, Longmans 1928.

6. In applying the concept of organism to the manhood of Christ, Thornton is seeking a way out of the difficulties raised by the two nature approach with its corollary of impersonal manhood. He seeks to avoid both adoptionism and monophysitism with this concept of organism. For a fuller discussion see J. M. Creed, 'Recent Tendencies in English Christology', *Mysterium Christi*, ed. G. K. A. Bell and D. A. Deissmann, Longmans 1924.

7. See N. Pittenger, *Christology Reconsidered*, SCM Press 1970, p. 19. Compare comments by J. Macquarrie, *Twentieth-Century Religious Thought*, SCM Press 1963, pp. 270ff.

8. P. Hamilton, *The Living God and the Modern World*, Hodder and Stoughton 1967, pp. 205ff., who therefore speaks of the uniqueness of Jesus Christ as his 'extreme specialness', a specialness which lay in the importance of his particular situation and role, in the way he accepted that role which led to his death, and especially in what happened after death ('the most outstandingly unique feature in the total event'). See also Hamilton's 'Some Proposals for a Modern Christology', *Christ For Us Today*, ed. N. Pittenger, SCM Press 1968. See also J. E. Barnhart, 'Incarnation and Process Philosophy', *Religious Studies* 2, 1966, pp. 225–32.

9. N. Pittenger, op. cit., p. 67. Compare also *The Word Incarnate*, Nisbet 1959, and 'The Doctrine of Christ in a Process Theology', *Expository Times*, October 1970, p. 8. Pittenger understands the divinity of Christ as an act of God which involved mutual prehensions (God acts through loving persuasion not coercion) and so preserves the humanity of Jesus.

10. Teilhard de Chardin, *Science and Christ*, Collins 1968, pp. 34ff., and *The Phenomenon of Man*, Fontana 1965, p. 296. See also C. Sykes, 'Teilhard de Chardin and the Cosmic Christ', *Theology*, 1975, p. 467. Teilhard is aware of the pantheistic danger inherent in relating creation and incarnation too closely. He therefore argues that it is 'the presence of the Incarnate Word [which] penetrates everything, as a universal element' (*Science and Christ*, p. 57).

11. *Science and Christ*, p. 165.

12. K. Rahner, 'Current Problems in Christology', *Theological Investigations*, Vol. I, Darton, Longman and Todd 1974, pp. 149–200; 'Christology Within an Evolutionary View of the World', Vol. V, Darton, Longman and Todd 1966, pp. 157–92, and *Foundations of Christian Faith*, Darton, Longman and Todd 1978, esp. ch. VI. Rahner argues that we are entirely justified in understanding creation

and incarnation 'not as two disparate and juxtaposed acts of God "outwards" which have their origins in two separate initiatives of God', but 'as two movements and two phases of the *one* process of God's self-giving and self-expression, although it is an intrinsically differentiated process' (*Foundations*, p. 197).

13. R. E. Doud, 'Rahner's Christology: A Whiteheadian Critique', *Journal of Religion*, 1977, p. 152, welcomes Rahner's contribution but believes that his thought needs a good dose of process philosophy in order to provide it with the metaphysical framework it lacks.

14. *Foundations*, p. 184.

15. *Foundations*, p. 220. Compare E. L. Mascall, who rejects process thought and is clear that 'neither the Incarnation nor anything else can involve any change in God himself' (*Christ, the Christian and the Church*, p. 14).

16. See T. F. Torrance, *Space, Time and Incarnation*, Oxford University Press 1969, especially Chapter 3, who argues that understanding the incarnation in the same way as creation preserves the act of God in space and time.

17. W. R. Matthews, *The Problem of Christ*, especially pp. 63ff.

18. N. Hook, *Christ in the Twentieth Century*, Lutterworth 1968, pp. 75f. Hook seeks a term which would not suggest two centres of consciousness and selects 'unitary consciousness', but the term does little more than express his desire not to suggest two centres.

19. P. Tillich, *Systematic Theology*, Vol. III, Nisbet 1964, p. 303.

20. See N. Ferré, 'Tillich and the Nature of Transcendence', ed. T. A. Kantonen, *Retrospect and Future*, Abingdon Press, Nashville 1964, p. 671, who recounts an occasion when Tillich agreed he should rethink his whole work in terms of the category of Spirit. Elsewhere Ferré has argued that Tillich could have begun with Christ as Agape and found the God who is personal Spirit ('Three Critical Issues in Tillich's Philosophical Theology', *Scottish Journal of Theology* 10, 1957, p. 237). See also D. Kelsey, *The Fabric of Paul Tillich's Theology*, Yale University Press 1967, who argues that the living God as Spirit is the ultimate synthesis to which the dialectic of being and existence points, and that 'God' and 'Spirit' are entirely interchangeable in Tillich's thought (pp. 160ff.).

21. Compare Lactantius, who, in the second half of the third century, uses the word *spiritus* so much for the issuing of the Son from the Father that his Logos doctrine becomes a Spirit christology. See A. Grillmeier, *Christ in Christian Tradition*, p. 197, who points out that Lactantius' thought, however, is pre-Nicene, that is, binitarian not trinitarian.

22. P. Tillich, 'Afterward: Appreciation and Reply', *Paul Tillich and Catholic Thoughts*, ed. T. A. O'Meara and C. D. Weisser, Darton, Longman and Todd 1965.

23. *Systematic Theology*, Vol. II, p. 156.

24. *Systematic Theology*, Vol. III, p. 153. Compare *Systematic Theology*, Vol. I, Nisbet 1953, p. 151.

25. G. W. H. Lampe, 'The Holy Spirit and the Person of Christ', *Christ, Faith and History*, p. 115. See also id., 'The Essence of Christianity: A Personal View', in *Explorations in Theology* 8, SCM Press 1981, pp. 119-30, and, especially, *God as Spirit*, Oxford University Press 1977.

26. Lampe insists that Spirit christology must not be understood in such a

way as to prevent Christ from being seen as the archetype and originator of the new community. But he sees this new community as Spirit-possessed and does not particularly relate it to the resurrection, as does the New Testament. Rather, the resurrection is somewhat bypassed in Lampe's exposition.

27. *God as Spirit*, p. 11.

28. Ibid., p. 61.

29. The relation between the models of incarnation and inspiration is discussed fully in C. F. D. Moule's *The Holy Spirit*, Mowbrays 1978, Chapter V, which, although not a direct reply to Lampe's *God As Spirit*, nevertheless argues forcibly for an absolute distinction between the two models. Moule does this primarily to ensure the absolute uniqueness of the incarnate Christ. But much of what he says is not directly applicable to Lampe's theological Spirit christology, for Lampe is not talking about an inspired person; he is propounding a Spirit christology with an ontological dimension. It may, however, be true that his persistent use of the model of inspiration is somewhat misleading, for his christology clearly amounts to more than this. (Further to Moule's argument, however, early Spirit christology does not altogether support his absolute distinction, for early Spirit christology was not necessarily conceived as non-incarnational: see J. N. D. Kelly, *Early Christian Doctrines*, A. and C. Black 1960, p. 143, for comments on the christology of Ignatius.)

30. *God as Spirit*, p. 24. Compare 'The Holy Spirit and the Person of Christ', p. 117, where Lampe similarly speaks of 'the raising of his humanity to its full potential, the completion of the human creation by the re-creating influence of the creator-Spirit'. This notion of continuous creation, of which salvation is a part, shows that the distinction Lampe makes between God's essence and his activity does not correspond to a distinction between incarnation and inspiration. For clearly God does not save by inspiration; salvation is part of that activity which is an expression of his essence.

31. 'The Essence of Christianity', p. 127.

32. So W. R. Matthews, *The Problem of Christ*, p. 83.

33. Indeed, Lampe wishes to stress that the historical figure was conditioned by the culture of his time and space, and therefore quite explicitly raises the difficult question of how an authentic, historical culture-conditioned figure can become the archetype of the relation of all men everywhere at all times to God (*God as Spirit*, p. 103).

34. Tillich here reflects Origen's belief that 'the soul of the man Jesus has received the Logos completely' (Origen, *Contra Celsum*, IV, ed. H. Chadwick, Cambridge University Press 1953, p. 47). In Origen's thought, the human 'soul' was the point of union; for Tillich, this was the human spirit. For Origen, the Logos took over the soul of Jesus; for Tillich, the Spirit took over the spirit of the man.

Conclusion

1. W. Herrmann, *The Communion of the Christian with God*, Crown Theological Library, 1906, reprinted SCM Press 1972.

2. See D. F. Strauss, *Life of Jesus*, London 1895, reprinted SCM Press 1972.

PART TWO

Chapter 4

1. C. F. D. Moule, 'The Manhood of Christ in the New Testament', *Christ, Faith and History*, p. 96.

2. H. P. Owen, 'The New Testament and the Incarnation: A Study in Doctrinal Development', *Religious Studies*, 8, 1972, p. 228.

3. Compare M. Black, *A Survey of Christological Thought, 1872–1972*, St Andrew Press, 1972. See also E. Schillebeeckx, *Jesus*, p. 53.

4. See, for example, J. D. G. Dunn, *Unity and Diversity*, SCM Press 1977, and *Christology in the Making*, SCM Press 1980.

5. See 'The Christian and the Bible', *Christian Believing* (Doctrinal Commission of the Church of England), SPCK 1976, p. 29. There are exceptions to this attitude, but it is generally to be found among those christologies I have discussed. There were exceptions, too, to the earlier response, such as Origen who believed that the significance of Jesus cannot be confined to a single lapidary statement and that the various New Testament titles illustrate the way in which those who live in communion with the face of Jesus see him in different ways – a very modern view! See A. Nichols, *The Art of God Incarnate*, Darton, Longman and Todd 1980, p. 65.

6. G. Stanton, 'Incarnational Christology in the New Testament', *Incarnation and Myth*, who argues that Paul's *kyrios* christology expresses the authority of the Lord over the individual and the Christian community, while his Son of God christology expresses the close relationship between God and Jesus and God's initiative in redemption (p. 164).

7. What C. F. D. Moule, *The Birth of the New Testament*, A. and C. Black 1966, calls a plurality of formulations of what happened in Jesus Christ (p. 9). Compare W. Pannenberg, *Jesus – God and Man*, SCM Press 1968. For the way this is worked out in worship, see G. Wainwright, *Doxology*, Epworth Press 1980, p. 282.

8. See R. H. Fuller, *The Foundations of New Testament Christology*, Fontana Books 1969, as opposed to O. Cullmann's *Christology of the New Testament*, SCM Press 1959, who interprets the New Testament christology in functional terms. We may not accept Fuller's detailed schematization, and we cannot accept his distinction between Palestinian and Hellenistic thought (see M. Hengel, *Judaism and Hellenism*, SCM Press 1974), but his book has confirmed the presence of an ontological dimension to much New Testament thought. See E. Schillebeeckx, *Jesus*, who argues that the very use of functional titles raises the question of who this Jesus is in himself, if all this is supposed to have happened in and through him 'as from God' (p. 547). Compare G. Dix, *Jew and Greek*, Dacre Press 1953, who argues that the function of the Messiah is the divine function (p. 80).

9. M. Hengel, *The Son of God*, SCM Press 1976, p. 92.

10. E. Schillebeeckx, *Jesus*, p. 62.

11. E. F. Scott, *The Apologetic of the New Testament*, William and Norgate 1907.

12. F. Young, 'A Cloud of Witnesses', *The Myth of God Incarnate*, p. 30.

13. P. Tillich, *Systematic Theology*, Vol. I, p. 8, who acknowledges that a commitment to the apologetic nature of theology such as he undertakes in his systematic theology needs to be matched with a recognition of the danger that the Christian message might be so adapted to the modern mind as to lose its essential and unique character. This would be to abandon the real apologetic task, as it is reflected in the New Testament.

14. See, for example, W. D. Davies and D. Daube (eds.), *The Background of the New Testament and Its Eschatology: Studies in Honour of C. H. Dodd*, Cambridge University Press 1956; R. P. C. Hanson, *The Significance of the Doctrine of the Last Things for Christian Belief*, John Rylands Library 1979, and F. Hahn, *The Titles of Jesus in Christology, Their History in Early Christianity*, Lutterworth Press 1969, who refers to the New Testament's 'consistently eschatological orientation' (p. 347). Compare G. Stanton, 'Incarnational Christology in the New Testament', *Incarnation and Myth*, pp. 151–66.

15. This is not to plead for a particular eschatology, nor to suppose that there is a single biblical eschatology. There is much diversity in the eschatological thought of the New Testament; indeed the doctrine itself was in movement (C. F. Evans, 'Unity and Pluriformity', *Christian Believing*, p. 51). For example, the eschatological framework of Mark 13 or I Thess. 4 is very different from that of Ephesians 4 or John 14–17. John's Gospel may suggest a receding of more primitive eschatology through the development of Logos thought and the recognition of the presence of judgment and salvation in the ministry of Jesus, and Paul's thought may have become less obviously eschatological in character, but a basic eschatological mood remains.

16. It is particularly important to recognize the eschatological character of the resurrection in the New Testament. See E. Schillebeeckx, *Jesus*, p. 360, who interprets the confession of Thomas as both eschatological in itself and as the beginnings of christology proper. The resurrection is an acknowledgment that in Jesus Christ the presence of God is to be found, 'the recognition of Jesus as the eschatological presence of God among us'. Compare the role of the resurrection in Pannenberg's thought, and see also K. Rahner, *Foundations*, p. 279, who argues that it was at the resurrection that it became fully manifest that Jesus of Nazareth was the absolute saviour. Those christologies which give little significance to the resurrection, dismissing it as culturally conditioned and incidental to the real meaning of Jesus, are neglecting not only that basic feature of the New Testament which constitutes the explicit Christian confession (so C. F. D. Moule, *The Origin of Christology*), but also an important expression of the eschatological character of the Christian faith.

17. So E. Schillebeeckx, *Jesus*, p. 56. Compare K. Rahner, *Foundations*, pp. 299ff., who says that the model of incarnation captures this and expresses the ultimacy and non-provisional character of God's act in Jesus Christ.

18. The recognition of the importance of eschatology does not, however, suggest a static understanding of christology. For New Testament eschatology is dynamic in character: it looks for a completion of what is, through God's intervention. A static christology is not able to reflect this note. What is suggested, therefore, is a more dynamic understanding of the incarnation, a more dynamic ontology.

19. This is not in conflict with the claim (note 16) of the non-provisional nature of God's action in Christ. For the action, on God's behalf, is non-provisional; the knowledge, on man's part, is bound to be provisional.

20. P. Tillich, *Perspectives*, pp. 91f., and *Systematic Theology*, Vol. I, pp. 6ff. See also A. Grillmeier, *Christ in Christian Tradition*, pp. 8f., who shows that in the immediate post-New Testament period, patristic theology illustrates the role of all theology in seeking to specify the relationship between the inherited kerygma and the need for a contemporary presentation. He judges that the very continuity of the theological struggles of the patristic age is to be found in its attempts to express the central question of the person of Christ and his uniqueness.

21. See C. F. D. Moule, *The Origin of Christology*, Cambridge University Press 1977, and M. Wiles, *The Remaking of Christian Doctrine*, SCM Press 1974, and the literature referred to in these works.

22. Both can be criticized as failing to expect radical change and for viewing the history of Christian doctrine as more or less a unified process of growth. As an alternative, N. Lash (*Change in Focus*, Sheed and Ward 1973, p. 144) advances a 'more episodic view of history' in which the continuities are more difficult to discern. Compare M. Foucault, *Archaeology of Knowledge*, Tavistock Publications 1972, and M. Bévenot, 'Primacy and Development', *Heythrop Journal* IX, 1968, pp. 400–13.

23. Compare the question of doctrinal development discussed by M. Wiles, *The Making of Christian Doctrine*, Cambridge University Press 1967. See also W. O. Chadwick, *From Bossuet to Newman*, Cambridge University Press 1957; J. Pelikan, *Historical Theology: Continuity and Change in Christian Doctrine*, Hutchinson 1971; and L. S. Thornton, *The Incarnate Lord*. See also J. M. Creed's discussion (*The Divinity of Jesus Christ*, p. 138) of whether the doctrine of the cosmic Christ is a right development from the earliest form of faith.

24. D. Cupitt, 'Professor Stanton on Incarnational Language in the New Testament', *Incarnation and Myth*, p. 167.

25. I have already referred to the twofold order of being, according to the flesh and according to the Spirit, in the discussion of Spirit christology. Tillich's basic dogma 'Jesus as the Christ', derived from the norm 'the New Being in Jesus as the Christ', is another example. Most attempts, however, advance little further than the basic common factor of the various New Testament expressions, namely, Jesus Christ. For a fuller discussion of the problems attached to the model of translation see, for instance, J. H. Thomas, *Paul Tillich: An Appraisal*, SCM Press 1963, p. 177, and D. Kelsey, *The Uses of Scripture in Recent Theology*, SCM Press 1975, p. 188.

26. Suggested, respectively, by D. Kelsey, op. cit., p. 189, M. Wiles, *Remaking*, pp. 7ff. (compare M. Lash, *Change in Focus*, p. 153), and E. Schillebeeckx, *Jesus*, p. 575.

27. See M. Wiles, *The Making of Christian Doctrine*, p. 173, and N. Lash, op. cit., ch. 15. The concept can be applied to the New Testament as well as to later Christian doctrine, see D. G. A. Calvert, 'Paul Tillich and Biblical Theology', *Scottish Journal of Theology*, December 1976, pp. 517–34. For example, in support of the incarnational model it is argued that 'many strands of New Testament evidence are not far in intention from the convictions which lie

behind incarnational doctrine' (G. Stanton, 'Mr Cupitt on Incarnational Christology in the New Testament', *Incarnation and Myth*, p. 170). Compare A. T. Hanson, for the same obligation to preserve the intention of the writers: *Grace and Truth*, SPCK 1975, p. 76, and *Studies in Paul's Technique and Theology*, SPCK 1974, pp. 211ff.

28. For example, Arius and Athanasius argued about texts from Proverbs, esp. Prov. 8.22, and Athanasius quoted Jeremiah to establish the eternity of the Son (Athanasius, *Orationes Contra Arius*).

29. See R. P. C. Hanson, 'Biblical Exegesis in the Early Church', *The Cambridge History of the Bible*, ed. P. R. Ackroyd and C. F. Evans, Vol. I, Cambridge University Press 1970, and M. Santer, 'Scripture and the Councils', *Sobornost*, Series 7, Winter 1975, pp. 99f.

30. As does F. Young, 'A Cloud of Witnesses', *The Myth of God Incarnate*, p. 22.

Chapter 5

1. K. Rahner, *Foundations*, p. 229.

2. N. Pittenger, *Christology Reconsidered*, p. 22.

3. R. E. Brown, *Jesus, God and Man*, Geoffrey Chapman, 1968. P. van Buren, *The Secular Meaning of the Gospel*, SCM Press 1963.

4. See N. Pittenger, *Christology Reconsidered*, chapter 3, and R. Williamson, 'Hebrews 4.15 and the Sinlessness of Jesus', *Expository Times*, October 1974, p. 4. As a modern concern, interest in this issue was initiated by Schleiermacher, though in classical christology it is most associated with the debate over the theology of Apollinarius. The later Apollinarian demand was for a Christ incapable of sinning (though probably earlier only for an actual lack of sin: see Grillmeier, *Christ in Christian Tradition*, p. 36). Modern discussion of the sinlessness of Jesus has not advanced much beyond the suggestion that emerges in this early debate, namely, that the human soul of Christ can be preserved through his temptation and testing, while his sinlessness can be asserted through his victory over these trials.

5. N. Pittenger, op. cit., p. 51.

6. J. Meyendorff, *Christ in Eastern Thought*, p. 115. Compare K. Rahner, *Theological Investigations*, Vol. I, p. 184, who also stresses the 'openness' of human nature, describing anthropology as deficient christology: 'only someone who forgets that the essence of man . . . is to be unbounded can suppose that it is impossible for there to be a man, who, precisely by being a man in the fullest sense . . . is God's existence in the world.'

7. P. Tillich, *Systematic Theology*, Vol. II, p. 145.

8. For an account of the meaning and use of these terms, see Chapter 6.

9. W. Pannenberg, *Jesus – God and Man*. A further example of theological judgments on the New Testament material is found in Robinson's argument that, as Hebrews never calls Jesus perfect but uses the verbal form 'perfected', it is a progressive perfecting of Jesus' personal being through conflict and victory which emerges as the key New Testament understanding of his sinlessness (J. A. T. Robinson, *The Human Face of God*, pp. 88ff.).

10. H. P. Owen, 'The Person of Christ', *Religious Studies* 13, 1977, p. 492.

11. M. Kähler, *The So-Called Historical Jesus and the Historic, Biblical Christ*, Fortress Press 1964, esp. pp. 43, 46 and 121–2.

12. A. Schweitzer, *The Quest of the Historical Jesus*, A. and C. Black 1964.

13. G. Tyrell, *Christianity at the Crossroads*, Longmans 1909.

14. *Lessing's Theological Writings*, ed. H. Chadwick, A. and C. Black 1956. See E. Schillebeeckx, *Jesus*, pp. 583ff. for a discussion of 'the Lessing question', where he comments that one view that has emerged out of the post-enlightenment acceptance of Lessing's dictum is that Jesus is a catalyst for religious values, an example of religious experience, but that in no way can any universal conclusion be drawn from his life. Such a view does not see contemporary religious experiences as bound up with the person of Jesus, and argues that they should not be projected back on him. This is a clear rejection of the concept of a uniquely universal Christ and a clear statement that our present faith is not tied to historical judgments about Jesus Christ.

15. J. M. Robinson, *A New Quest of the Historical Jesus*, SCM Press 1959; E. Käsemann, 'The Problem of the Historical Jesus', *Essays on New Testament Themes*, SCM Press 1964.

16. J. Smart, *The Interpretation of Scripture*, SCM Press 1961, p. 85.

17. D. E. Nineham, 'Jesus in the Gospels', *Christ For Us Today*, ed. N. Pittenger, SCM Press 1968.

18. Paul Tillich, *Systematic Theology*, Vol. II, p. 118, and *Perspectives*, p. 227.

19. Kähler had no desire to detach christology from the historical existence of the man Jesus of Nazareth as the Bible portrays him. See C. E. Braaten, *History and Hermeneutics*, Lutterworth Press 1968, p. 61. Such continuity is asserted, too, by Kähler's disciple, Tillich, through his concept of an *analogia imaginis* between the picture and the person, *Systematic Theology*, Vol. II, p. 132.

20. Tillich therefore describes his theology as an 'attempt to draw out the consequences for systematic theology created by a sceptical attitude to the New Testament generally and to the historical Jesus in particular', (*Perspectives*, p. 227).

21. J. Moltmann, *The Crucified God*, SCM Press 1974, p. 84.

22. J. A. Baker, *The Foolishness of God*, Darton, Longman and Todd 1970, p. 137.

23. E. Schillebeeckx, *Jesus*, p. 65.

24. Compare J. Sobrino, *Christology at the Crossroads*, SCM Press 1978, p. 275.

25. Williams claims that as there is no portrait of Jesus the man, there is no sense in saying that in his human character we see the character of God (H. A. Williams, 'Incarnation: Model and Symbol', *Theology*, January 1976, p. 8). Yet he still claims that Jesus is a model, or better still a symbol, of the relationship of God and man. He does this on the basis of how Jesus is set before us in the gospel presentation, making a distinction similar to Tillich's distinction between the historical figure and the biblical picture. It is not sufficient, however, to work only with the biblical picture; there is a proper and necessary role for historical investigation. That role, however, must not be exaggerated.

26. For example, D. Welbourn, *God-Dimensional Man*, Epworth Press 1972, p. 84, claims that 'Jesus is personally unique in that he is the first man in whom human potentiality (in the moral sense) has reached complete fulfilment'. This

appears to be a judgment resting on historical investigation. But the New Testament does not so treat the question. John's Gospel does express the unity of Jesus with the Father in moral terms, but in so doing is making an essentially theological judgment, expressed in terms of the unity of the will. It is not a judgment based on historical investigation.

27. E. Schillebeeckx, *Jesus*, p. 72, writes: 'There is a continual interaction between remembering and later experiences; detailed reminiscences modify the total picture of Jesus that lives in the community; and those memories are classified in the light of the complete life of Jesus.'

28. R. Butterworth, 'Bishop Robinson and Christology', *Religious Studies* 11, 1975, p. 79.

29. H. Meynell, *New Theology and Modern Theologians*, Sheed and Ward 1967, p. 130. Compare E. L. Mascall, *Secularization of Christianity*, Darton, Longman and Todd 1965, pp. 245ff. See also P. Carnley, 'The Poverty of Historical Scepticism', *Christ, Faith and History*, p. 189, for the general argument.

30. Tillich argues that faith's risk concerns the totality of our being, but excludes the risk of historicity, *Systematic Theology*, Vol. II, p. 134. For the opposite view to this, see R. Hepburn, *Christianity and Paradox*, Watts 1967, chapter 6 and 7.

31. Even the most sceptical are limited in their scepticism. Bultmann accepts the historicity of the life of Jesus and his death on the cross and offers quite specific details in his reconstruction of the historical Jesus. See R. Bultmann, 'The Primitive Christian Kerygma and the Historical Jesus', ed. C. E. Braaten and R. A. Harrisville, *The Historical Jesus and the Kerygmatic Christ*, Abingdon Press, Nashville 1964. See also A. E. Harvey, *Jesus and the Constraints of History*, Duckworth 1982, for illustrations of the way in which New Testament scholars have moved away from the scepticism of the form-critical period.

32. J. S. Dunne, *A Search for God in Time and Memory*, Sheldon Press 1975, p. 8. U. Simon, 'The Multidimensional Picture of Jesus', in *What About the New Testament?*, ed. M. D. Hooker and C. Hickling, SCM Press 1975.

33. A. Grillmeier, *Christ in Christian Tradition*, p. 5. This seeks to distinguish what can be known by strictly historical methods from any discernible alteration or touching up to which the historical figure has been subjected. See G. Ebeling, *Word and Faith*, SCM Press 1963, p. 294.

34. See A. Grillmeier's comments on Lactantius, *Christ in Christian Tradition*, p. 191.

35. E. Schillebeeckx, *Jesus*, p. 636.

Chapter 6

1. P. Tillich, *Christianity and the Encounter of World Religions*, Columbia University Press 1963, who argues that the Christian religion makes no exclusive claims about itself, and does not negate other religions it encounters. On the contrary, it affirms the revelatory experience in other religions through the universal principle of self-manifestation, namely, the Logos.

2. G. Rupp, *Christologies and Culture: Towards a Typology of Religious World Views*, Mouton, The Hague 1974, pp. 199ff., argues that Rahner's christo-

centricism appears to deny the possibility of God working outside the person of Christ, whereas his general sympathy with evolutionary thought suggests an acceptance of this possibility. He suggests that Rahner's concept of the anonymous Christian (one who experiences grace but does not experience grace as grace) indicates that he limits salvation to Christ. In my view the danger is that such christocentricism can prevent the recognition that the work of Christ is really the work of the universal God.

3. J. V. Taylor, 'The Theological Basis of Inter-faith Dialogue', J. Hick and B. Hebblethwaite (eds.), *Christianity and Other Religions*, Fontana Books 1980, pp. 212–33.

4. See P. Tillich, *Systematic Theology*, Vol. II, p. 110; id., *Perspectives*, pp. 112–13; and C. F. D. Moule, 'Is Christ Unique?', *Fact, Faith and Fantasy*, Fontana Books 1964, p. 112.

5. M. Wiles, 'Looking Into the Sun', *Working Papers in Doctrine*, p. 155.

6. See F. Young, 'Incarnation and Atonement: God Suffered and Died', *Incarnation and Myth*, p. 103; and B. Hebblethwaite, 'Incarnation and Atonement: The Moral and Religious Value of the Incarnation', *Incarnation and Myth*, p. 98.

7. P. C. Mozoomdar, *Spirit of God*, Boston, Mass. 1894, quoted by M. M. Thomas, *The Acknowledged Christ of the Indian Renaissance*, SCM Press 1969, p. 89, asserts the uniqueness of Christ on the ground that 'he completes all other partial and local incarnations and makes for a truly spiritual and universal incarnation of the Spirit, and provides an everlasting model of the divine order of humanity'. He speaks of man's need for a central figure who includes in himself all these various embodiments of God's self-manifestation, and identifies this as a need for 'an incarnation in which all other incarnations will be completed'. This Indian use of incarnation is very much broader than the typical Western usage.

8. See D. M. Baillie, *God Was in Christ*, pp. 174f., who relates the Christian experience of God's grace at work within a person's life to the mystery of the incarnation, treating the incarnation as a similar paradox, taken at the perfect and absolute pitch.

9. J. A. T. Robinson, *The Human Face of God*, p. 140.

10. N. Pittenger, *Christology Reconsidered*, pp. 116f. A difference in degree, it is argued, avoids any anomaly by denying that God's indwelling in Jesus differs in kind from his indwelling in other men.

11. H. P. Owen, 'The New Testament and the Incarnation: A Study in Doctrinal Development', *Religious Studies* 8, 1972, p. 221.

12. Compare D. M. Mackinnon, ' "Substance" in Christology', *Christ, Faith and History*, p. 292. Some degree christology is content with an assertion of the ordinariness of Jesus' humanity and so does not wish it to accept the weight of christology. This is not the way in which Chalcedon speaks, for its *vere deus, vere homo* in one person claims uniqueness for both natures (see Pannenberg, *Jesus: God and Man*, p. 284).

13. If it is argued that the difference in degree is so great as to become virtually a difference in kind (W. Temple, *Christus Veritas*, Macmillan 1944, p. 147, n. 1; N. Pittenger, *Christology Reconsidered*, p. 112), we are not really dealing with degree christology at all.

14. E. Schillebeeckx, *Jesus*, pp. 597ff.; K. Rahner, *Foundations*, pp. 198ff.

15. See my later discussion of the terms 'active' and 'present'.

16. A. J. Toynbee, *Christianity Among the Religions of the World*, Oxford University Press 1958.

17. J. Hick, *God and the Universe of Faiths*, Macmillan 1973; see also 'Christ's Uniqueness', *Reform*, October 1974, pp. 18–19.

18. For example, K. Jaspers, *The Great Philosphers*, Hart-Davis 1962, pp. 105ff., who argues that historical and temporal reality, by the very fact that it is historical, cannot be universally valid for all mankind: Jesus, as a historical figure, has his limitations. He does not, however, wish to deny all uniqueness or universality. He views Jesus as one who is illumined by the Godhead, who transcends the world, whose orientation towards the transcendent put everything in the world in question. In his estimate, Jesus is the unique cipher of the transcendent, but he is not the exclusive God-man. Compare his *Truth and Symbol*, Vision Press 1959, pp. 76ff. See also H. A. Durfee, 'Karl Jaspers' Christology', *Journal of Religion*, Vol. XLIV, 1964, 133–47, and P. A. Schlipp, *The Philosophy of Karl Jaspers*, New York 1957.

19. C. F. D. Moule, 'Is Christ Unique?', p. 107. Compare D. Welbourn, *God-Dimensional Man*, and J. Lipner, 'Christians and the Uniqueness of Christ', *Scottish Journal of Theology* 28, 1975, p. 359.

20. See, for example, J. Knox, *The Death of Christ*, Fontana Books 1967, p. 125: the uniqueness of Jesus was the absolute uniqueness of what God did in him.

21. Such is the criticism often levelled, for instance, at Tillich's christology. In so far as it is an event christology, the cross is singled out as the one event of supreme significance, because it is seen as a test of his unity with God. Even the cross, however, in Tillich's exposition, has no factual element except 'the surrender of him who is called the Christ to the ultimate consequences of existence' (*Systematic Theology*, Vol. ii, p. 179).

22. Compare J. Ziesler, *The Jesus Question*, Lutterworth Press 1980, p. 116.

23. See S. Ogden's existential understanding of how God acts ('What does it mean to say 'God Acts in History?', in *The Reality of God*, SCM Press 1967, pp. 164–87) where God's decisive act means '*that* understanding of human existence which is, in fact, the ultimate truth about our life before God'. See M. Wiles, *Working Papers*, pp. 139ff., who speaks only in terms of man's greater responsiveness and is able to say about the life of Jesus only that this particular story has been a source of inspiration.

24. One of the problems of an event-christology is that it invites a modern scientific reaction which sees any alleged post-creation action as interventionist. This view would need correction, for God is not at one remove from his world and set in a somewhat deistic relation to it. Event christology, however, does not easily provide the necessary correction.

25. Compare G. Wainwright, *Doxology*, Epworth Press 1980, p. 82, who examines the personal character of the functions performed in the sacraments and likens them to the christological category of presence.

26. Spirit christology can be expressed either in terms of event or person, or both. Lampe's thought stresses what God did through the life of Jesus and denies that the presence of God in Jesus was any different from his presence in

anyone else. Tillich, in his later thought, places more emphasis on Jesus' unique possession of the Spirit and thereby stresses God's initiative rather than man's responsiveness.

27. The category of presence is much more akin to the Elohist understanding of God's intervention from within than the Yahwistic intervention from outside. See P. Schoonenberg, *The Christ*.

28. M. Wiles, 'Looking Into the Sun', *Working Papers*, p. 156, who argues that if your overall view of the world and of God's dealing with it looks for some final cataclysmic event which will bring the whole process to its destined goal, then the work of the one who brings in that event will be seen as distinct in kind from others who have gone before him. Wiles does not himself extend this to the person of Christ, only to his work, and wishes in any case to abandon the whole concept of ultimacy because he sees it culturally tied to a certain eschatological view.

29. C. F. D. Moule, 'The Distinctiveness of Christ', *Theology*, November 1973, p. 566. Compare J. Riches, *Jesus and the Transformation of Judaism*, Darton, Longman and Todd 1980.

30. J. A. T. Robinson, *Truth is Two-Eyed*, SCM Press 1979, especially chapter V.

31. A. T. Hanson, *Grace and Truth*, ch. 4.

PART THREE

Chapter 7

1. Even at its best, its tendency is to treat Jesus as the clue to the mystery of the Christ, but not to take seriously the implication of the confession that Christ is the clue to the mystery of God. See N. Lash, 'Interpretation and Imagination', *Incarnation and Myth*, p. 24, who writes that it almost seems as if christological problems 'are not problems about the meaning of "God" at all, which is odd'.

2. This is ironical in the light of Rahner's description of the two types of christology as 'saving type' and 'metaphysical' ('The Two Basic Types of Christology', *Theological Investigations*, Vol. 13, Darton, Longman and Todd 1975, pp. 213–23).

3. Schillebeeckx is right to call for a recognition of the Christian status of each type by the other as a basis for dialogue among Christians (*Jesus*, p. 30). Much Christian thinking has of course recognized these two sides, as the very term 'Jesus Christ' suggests. For example, Tillich expresses the basic twofoldnesses of christology when he speaks of Jesus as the Christ as both an historical fact and a subject of believing reception (*Systematic Theology*, Vol. II, p. 113). Moltmann, too, in a rather different way speaks of a fixed point and a historically changeable one: Jesus and his history remain fixed but the titles are historically changeable, a response to his openness (*The Crucified God*, pp. 106ff.). See also K. Popper's arguments against opting only for one model (*Conjectures and Refutations*, Routledge and Kegan Paul 1972).

4. The distinction made between historical and doxological statements illustrates our position. Historical statements are made about God's relationship to, or activity in, some historical event. The doxological statements make an

affirmation more directly about God himself. Christological statements are both historical and doxological. Christology needs to recover this double perspective. See E. Schlink, *The Coming Christ and the Coming Church*, who emphasizes the doxological character of doctrine.

5. J. Moltmann, for example, seeks to achieve precisely this in arguing that 'when the crucified Jesus is called the "image of the invisible God", the meaning is that *this* is God, and that God is like *this*'. However, he largely confines this approach to the cross and does not follow through the implication of his statements that God is like this in other areas. His use of a modified kenotic model prevents the full impact on the doctrine of God.

6. This is why Schillebeeckx claims that Jesus was and is 'aspectivally' both the definitive parable of God and the definitive paradigm of humanity (*Jesus*, p. 604).

7. So H. Küng, *On Being a Christian*, Collins 1977, p. 442. Küng recognizes this to be so when he writes that 'it is a God of powerlessness who humanizes man and makes possible his freedom', for it is only in discovering the God of powerlessness that we are able to apply this theological insight to our understanding of humanity.

8. N. Richardson, *Was Jesus Divine?*, Epworth Press 1979, p. 47.

9. See J. A. Baker, *The Foolishness of God*, pp. 188ff., for a fuller discussion of what Jesus said about God. See also J. Riches, *Jesus and the Transformation of Judaism*, for an examination of the way Jesus modified the conventional understanding of the nature and activity of God. See J. Jeremias, *The Prayers of Jesus*, SCM Press 1967, for a discussion of Jesus' use of *abba*.

10. See C. F. D. Moule, *The Origin of Christology*, p. 138.

11. J. M. Creed, *The Divinity of Jesus Christ*, p. 119. Nicaea and Chalcedon achieved a certain objective, but their results were expressed within the framework of a pre-Christian understanding of God and this was what their christology therefore confirmed. Even there, however, it was recognized that christological confessions were really affirmations about God (compare Schillebeeckx, *Jesus*, p. 56). Unfortunately, their implications were not followed through, and there was no break with inherited theological thinking. God was not conceived differently as a result of their affirmation of the divinity of Christ. Attention instead was centred on the question of the one undivided Christ. Subsequent christology has, for the most part, merely worked over the same ground, rehearsing arguments for the divinity of Christ and the unity of his person.

12. Despite a widespread recognition of this theological task, there is general unwillingness to allow the necessary theological revision. For example, Montefiore limits christology to clarifying and defining but not altering the concept of God (H. Montefiore, in *Essays in Christian Believing*, A Report of the Doctrine Commission of the Church of England, SPCK 1976, p. 151). Hodgson recognizes that the decisions up to Nicaea showed Christians trying to fit the new evidence provided by Christ into their existing categories of Godhead, but himself fails to abandon the inherited concept of God's impassibility, preferring to explain how it is limited in both creation and incarnation (L. Hodgson, *For Faith and Freedom*, SCM Press 1968, Vol. II, pp. 8off.). Pannenberg argues that 'the distinctiveness of the christological way of speaking about Jesus resides in its theological

character' (*Jesus*, p. 19), but in practice presupposes the idea of God 'historically and in substance'. His theology from below carries with it the chief presuppositions of a theology from above, namely, knowledge of the concept of God.

13. See M. Hengel, *Judaism and Hellenism*, SCM Press 1974. Nor do I dispute M. Wiles's judgment (*The Spiritual Gospel*, Cambridge University Press 1960, p. 158) that while 'later scholars may point with justice to the influence of Greek metaphysical thought upon their writings and their understanding of the Gospel ... in conscious aim and intention their overriding purpose was to interpret the message of the Bible'.

14. J. N. D. Kelly, *Early Christian Doctrines*, A. and C. Black 1960, p. 87: 'The doctrine of one God ... was her bulwark against paganism, Gnostic emanationism and Marcionite dualism.' Compare K. Ward, *The Concept of God*, Blackwell 1974, who argues that the development of the non-duality of God is the most important feature of the early Christian concept of God.

15. R. A. Norris, *God and the World in Early Christian Theology*, A. and C. Black 1966, p. 135, comments that one result of dialogue of Christian faith with Greek philosophy was 'the formulation of an idea of God, which, at its very centre, embraced a fundamental tension between the ideals of an immortal Perfection beyond the world and a creative sovereignty in and over it'.

16. J. Milet, *God or Christ?*, SCM Press 1981. Compare W. Thüsing, *A New Christology*, K. Rahner and W. Thüsing, Burns and Oates 1980, pp. 93ff.

17. C. F. Evans, 'Christology and Theology', *Explorations in Theology* 2, SCM Press 1977, who argues that in those letters addressed specifically to Gentiles faith in one God is commended in the face of popular paganism.

18. For a recent discussion of some of the difficult questions associated with the biblical experience of Christ, see E. Schillebeeckx, *Christ: The Christian Experience in the Modern World*, SCM Press 1980.

19. Compare J. V. Taylor, 'The Theological Basis of Inter-faith Dialogue', Hick and Hebblethwaite (eds.), *Christianity and Other Religions*, p. 229, who says that 'if our idea of God differs in any respect from what we see in him ... then it is our idea of God that has to be changed', for once we have seen him, we could not find it in us to worship a God who was different.

20. J. Moltmann, *The Crucified God*, p. 88, who argues that the more the early church emphasized the divinity of Christ on the basis of this concept of God the more difficult it was to show that the Son of God was Jesus of Nazareth.

21. W. H. Vanstone, *Love's Endeavour, Love's Expense*, Darton, Longman and Todd 1977, pp. 72ff. Mascall's thought is an example of how the inherited doctrine of God determines the limits of christology. He says that 'in becoming incarnate the divine Word does not cease to exercise his divine functions as the eternally begotten Son of the Father' (E. L. Mascall, *Christ, the Christian and the Church*, p. 15).

22. See W. Pannenberg, *Jesus – God and Man*, pp. 307ff., for a fuller account of the usage of the term.

23. Variant forms of kenosis have been put forward in an attempt to meet some of these difficulties. For example, the concept of self-relinquishment is abandoned in favour of self-limitation of divine power (F. Weston, *The One Christ*, Longmans 1907), or accepting the limitations of manhood (C. Gore, *The Reconstruction of Belief*, and *The Incarnation of the Son of God*). Or, to cite

another variant, the renunciation of attributes is rejected in favour of a new mode of their being: a retraction of their mode of being from active to potential (P. T. Forsyth, *The Person and Place of Jesus Christ*, London 1909). But these theories suffer in principle from the major defect of working with a wrong concept of God. They fail to understand the Christian God christologically; their theories are unnecessary.

24. Even Moltmann is reluctant when it comes to ascribing Christ's suffering to God, and says that Jesus 'abandoned his divine identity and found his true identity in the cross' (*The Crucified God*, p. 16).

25. J. A. T. Robinson, *The Human Face of God*, quotes Grillmeier to this effect (*Christ in Christian Tradition*, p. 25), yet ends his book on the disappointing note of the anonymous Christ.

26. W. H. Vanstone, *Love's Endeavour, Love's Expense*, p. 58. Compare G. MacGregor, *He Who Lets Us Be: A Theology of Love*, Seabury Press, New York 1975, who uses the kenotic model for the totality of a God who is always self-humbling and self-limiting. The biblical foundation for these interpretations can be found in C. F. D. Moule's exposition of Philippians 2. For Moule suggests that, as the natural meaning of *harpagmos* is 'the act of grasping', v. 6 should be translated 'Jesus did not reckon equality with God in terms of snatching'. He suggests that the verse means that Jesus saw God-likeness essentially as giving and spending oneself-out (C. F. D. Moule, 'Further Reflections on Phil. 2.5–11', *Apostolic History and the Gospel*, ed. W. W. Gasque and R. P. Martin, Paternoster Press 1970; compare A. M. Ramsey, *Jesus and the Living Past*, Oxford University Press 1980, p. 39).

Chapter 8

1. See S. M. Ogden, *The Reality of God*, SCM Press 1967.

2. See, for example, L. Moonan, 'Why Can't God Do Everything?', *New Blackfriars*, December 1974, pp. 552–62.

3. J. Moltmann, *The Crucified God*, p. 223. I do not mean to suggest that the traditional view of God always stressed power over and against love. There has remained a clear stress on the love of God in the development of Christian doctrine, supported principally by the Johannine writings.

4. As expounded in terms of the South American situation in J. Sobrino, *Christology at the Crossroads*, p. 222. See also J. A. Baker, *The Foolishness of God*, p. 278. Sobrino and Baker are rather more interested in drawing conclusions about our understanding of man than pursuing this approach in a more strictly theological sense.

5. R. P. C. Hanson analyses the problem correctly when he says that the Fathers, blinded by their belief in God's impassibility, could not or would not recognize that God in Christ chose the way of weakness. But, sadly, he withdraws from the implications of his argument that as Jesus Christ is the self-communication of God we must remove the last remnant of Platonism from our Christian understanding of God. For he describes God as one who cannot fail and who was not taking a risk in the incarnation. In the end, Hanson's concept of God is kenotic (he chooses not to know and chooses to be limited in knowledge and power). This is the only way the god of antiquity can become human.

Hanson has allowed the revelation of God in Jesus Christ only partly to modify his prior concept of God and so has defeated the purposes of christological theology (see *The Attractiveness of God*, pp. 112f.).

6. C. F. D. Moule, 'The Manhood of Jesus in the New Testament', p. 99. Compare A. M. Ramsey's belief that 'the glory of Christ in the Passion is the mirror of God's own omnipotence', by which Ramsey means that in the face of the suffering and frustration of the world he can find belief in God's own sovereignty credible only in terms of sacrificial love (unpublished sermon at centenary of Lincoln Theological College, 11 June 1974).

7. J. Hick, *Evil and the God of Love*, Fontana Books 1968. Hick's theodicy is along Irenaean lines, with some modifications suggested by the Augustinian tradition. Augustine saw evil as the privation of good, stemming from the misuse of freedom. Irenaeus suggested that man was created imperfect, but intended for growth and perfection: the world of mingled good and evil is the necessary environment for such growth.

8. W. H. Vanstone, op. cit. Compare G. MacGregor's definition of divine power as that 'infinite power that springs from creative love', (p. 15).

9. Tertullian, *De Carne Christi*, 10. Origen, *Dialogue With Heraclides*. For its adoption by the Greeks, the Cappadocians and patristic theology in general, see Grillmeier, *Christ in Christian Tradition*, p. 115.

10. G. Aulén, *Christus Victor*, SPCK 1970. Aulén rejects both nineteenth-century liberalism and Anselm's approach to the atonement for basically the same reason: the atonement was not seen by either as God's work in the fullest sense.

11. L. Hodgson, *For Faith and Freedom*, Vol. II, p. 75.

12. A. T. and R. C. P. Hanson, *Reasonable Belief: A Survey of the Christian Faith*, Oxford University Press 1981, p. 108.

13. C. F. D. Moule, *The Sacrifice of Christ*, Hodder and Stoughton 1956, p. 39.

14. See D. L. Edwards, *God's Cross in our World*, SCM Press 1951, p. 113.

15. F. Young, *Sacrifice and the Death of Christ*, SPCK, 1975, p. 135.

16. K. Rahner, *Foundations*, pp. 192f., describes the saviour as both the absolute promise of God and the acceptance of this self-communication. This is how Rahner understands the hypostatic union.

17. Compare G. Wainwright, *Doxology*, pp. 57ff.

18. See R. P. C. Hanson, 'Introduction', 'Historical Theology', *Pelican Guide to Modern Theology*, Vol. II, Penguin Books 1969, who concludes that here the law of prayer decided the law of belief.

19. J. A. Jungmann, *The Early Liturgy*, Darton, Longman and Todd 1960, p. 195.

20. Compare W. Thüsing, *A New Christology*, p. 109, who argues that 'Jesus Christ . . . does not come between God and men . . . he makes it possible for God to be experienced directly'.

21. Tillich speaks of the mediator as a third being who is only a half-god who at the same time is half-man (*Systematic Theology*, Vol. II, pp. 107ff.) and seeks to correct the danger by speaking of Christ as essential man and essential God-manhood who is able to represent not only man to man but God to man, for 'essential man by his very nature represents God'.

22. If it be replied that much that calls itself mediator christology intends no more than to say that the Father has graciously provided that we may think of 'our Man' in heaven, rather than to deny that God himself is near us, then it would be less confusing for such theology not to call itself mediator christology. For the use of the term suggests a pattern of thought in which God and man are separated, except through the use of a mediator.

23. See J. A. Baker, *The Foolishness of God*, pp. 61ff., 384ff. Compare F. Young, *Sacrifice and the Death of Christ*, p. 136, who asks what sort of a God it is who likes to be told how marvellous he is and who changes his mind in our favour if we give him the promise of a good offering in return.

24. E. J. Tinsley, *The Imitation of God in Christ*, SCM Press 1960. See also 'Some Principles of Reconstructing a Doctrine of the Imitation of Christ', *Scottish Journal of Theology* 25, February 1972, p. 47.

Chapter 9

1. I. T. Ramsey, *Models and Mystery*, Oxford University Press 1964.
2. I have noted both the variety of models used in the New Testament and Popper's argument that a single model is necessarily deficient. There is therefore much to be said for seeking what H. A. Williams calls 'a mutually qualifying plurality of models of the incarnation' ('Incarnation: Model and Symbol', *Theology*, January 1976, p. 8).
3. So B. Hebblethwaite, 'Incarnation – the Essence of Christianity?', *Theology*, March 1977, p. 90.
4. G. Kittel, *Theological Dictionary of the New Testament* 3, Eerdmans 1966, pp. 563–92, s.v. *apokalypto, apokalypsis*.
5. This is supported by the distinction J. McIntyre (*The Shape of Christology*, SCM Press, pp. 145ff.) makes between the model of revelation in the Old Testament in which God reveals some aspect of his being or nature to some person, and in the New Testament where God does not just reveal one of his attributes, or even his whole purpose, but his very self. McIntyre argues therefore that some modification of the revelation model as it is used in the Old Testament is needed to accommodate the conviction that 'in having to do with God as he is in Christ, we have to do with God as he is in and for himself'. This modification turns the revelation model into the sort of disclosure model Ramsey identifies, and prevents the danger of seeing Christ as the 'image' of God, in the sense of an inferior disclosure, or as an emanation from the monad, as in Eusebius, *Demonstrato Evangelica*, V.8.
6. See J. Painter, *John, Witness and Theologian*, SPCK 1975, for a summary of the most important material in John's Gospel and for a full bibliography.
7. J. Baillie, *The Idea of Revelation in Recent Thought*, Oxford University Press 1956, p. 62.
8. L. Hodgson, *For Faith and Freedom*, SCM Press 1968.
9. Chiefly by G. Downing, *Has Christianity a Revelation?*, SCM Press 1964, part of whose argument is summarized in this paragraph. Downing attacks the confidence with which the term is used despite the wide variety of meaning attached to its content. He is especially critical of its use by N. Pittenger, D. M. Baillie and H. Montefiore.

10. Compare Aulén's treatment of Jesus as the one who reveals and the one who liberates. In both, he argues, Jesus is telling, in word and deed alike, of God who acts in a certain way and who therefore is like this (*Jesus*, p. 162). Compare A. Grillmeier, *Christ in Christian Tradition*, p. 27, who argues that Christ appears as the unique and absolute revealer, but that 'this activity of revelation is directed completely towards the *salvation* of men, for it brings life . . .' Compare K. Rahner, *Foundations*, pp. 144ff., who argues that there can be no separation between revelation and salvation because the history of salvation is also that of revelation. This has been well recognized whenever christology has been at its best. See Athanasius, *On the Incarnation*, where it is clear that without an assertion of the Godhead of Christ there could have been no full salvation: for the saviour to be perfectly adequate he must have been the revealer of God himself.

11. See A. T. Hanson, *Grace and Truth*, pp. 36ff., who argues that 'the nature of God is manifested in the complete humanity of Jesus Christ in a way which could not have been accomplished by some superhuman manifestations'. Hanson presents a christology of the divinity in the humanity, a christology from below which is heavily dependent on the concept of revelation. We recall Schoonenberg's distinction between intervention from within creation, as in the Elohist writings, and intervention from outside, as with the Yahwist. The concept of intervention from within is not a denial of God's revelation, rather is it an attempt to express revelation from below.

12. See D. Bonhoeffer, *Christology*, p. 103, who is unwilling to accept that it is sufficient to say that Christ is God's *prosopon*, the form in which God appears, precisely because that does not take revelation seriously. In modalism, God himself does not encounter man in Jesus Christ; only trinitarian thought permits that.

13. J. Moltmann, *The Crucified God*, p. 235.

14. B. Hebblethwaite, 'Incarnation and Atonement', p. 93.

15. A. Nichols, *The Art of God Incarnate*, suggests a renewal of the theology of revelation on the model of the artwork to produce an aesthetic theology of revelation. Here he suggests that as in art there is an unveiling which is at the same time a concealment, so revelation involves both. Compare E. J. Tinsley, 'Tell It Slant', *Theology*, May 1980, p. 169, who argues that all revelation is provisional in character.

16. Revelation is, however, the opposite to kenosis, though there is unveiling and concealing in both. For kenosis denies the basic assertion of a christology which seeks to express the essential self-communication of God in Jesus Christ, and does not lead to a re-interpretation of the triune God from a christological perspective. A choice therefore has to be made between revelation and kenosis.

Conclusion

1. J. Hick, *God and the Universe of Faiths*, Macmillan 1973.

Index

113

Wainwright, G., 87, 97, 104, 109
Ward, K., 107
Weisser, C. D., 95
Welbourn, D., 101, 104
Weston, F., 107
Whitehead, A. N., 19, 20, 21, 24, 94
Wiles, M., 87, 92, 93, 99, 103, 104, 105, 107
Williams, C. J. E., 92
Williams, H. A., 101, 110
Williamson, R., 100
world religions, 51–2, 53, 75, 78, 84, 102, 103
worship, 75–7

Young, F., 87, 93, 98, 100, 103, 109, 110

Ziesler, J., 104